GROW YOUR HANDMADE BUSINESS

How to Envision, Develop, and Sustain
a Successful Creative Business

KARI CHAPIN

Illustrations by
Jennifer Judd-McGee

Storey Publishing

The mission of Storey Publishing is to serve our customers by
publishing practical information that encourages
personal independence in harmony with the environment.

Edited by Deborah Balmuth and Dale Evva Gelfand
Art direction and book design by Alethea Morrison
Text production by Liseann Karandisecky
Illustrations by © Jennifer Judd-McGee/Lilla Rogers Studio
Indexed by Catherine Goddard

Storey Publishing
210 MASS MoCA Way
North Adams, MA 01247
www.storey.com

Printed in the United States by Versa Press
10 9 8 7 6 5 4 3 2 1

LIBRARY OF CONGRESS CATALOGING-IN-PUBLICATION DATA

Chapin, Kari.
  Grow your handmade business / by Kari Chapin.
    p. cm.
  Includes index.
  ISBN 978-1-60342-989-4 (pbk. : alk. paper)
  1. Handicraft industries—Management. 2. Handicraft—Marketing.
  3. Selling—Handicraft. I. Title.
HD9999.H362C528 2012
745.5068'4—dc23
                                                    2012004612

To my community.
We're all in this together.
Thank goodness.

CONTENTS

PART 2: PLANNING FOR SUCCESS

INTRODUCTION

The first time I wrote up a business plan was in 2005. My husband, Eric, and I were living in Alabama, and we desperately wanted to get back to our native New England. Problem was, we had no money to make the move. Eric's job had transferred us to Alabama, and we were stuck there, largely dependent on his salary and under contract to stay there for at least one year.

The fall of that Alabama year, I took a trip to Chicago to attend a conference for people passionate about public radio. At the time, I was following my dream of working somewhere in the field of public radio by doing low-paying (or no-paying!) freelance gigs, and while I was in Chicago, I interviewed a couple who owned one of the first cupcake-only bakeries in the United States. Even way back then, I enjoyed combining my love of fresh, new, creative businesses with my love of telling stories and helping people. My best friend, Karie, had tipped me off to this at-the-time-unusual business near her Chicago neighborhood. I was immediately smitten by the idea of a cupcakery and jumped at the chance to learn all I could about a bakery that sold only cupcakes.

I fell in love with the idea of owning my own cupcakery. When I got home, I excitedly told Eric all about my idea for a new kind of business. Then I got to work.

I devoted all of my time to researching and working on my baking skills and scheming. Oh, how I schemed! During the middle of all of this pre-enterprise enterprise, the owners of that Chicago bakery called me and asked if I might be interested in buying their business. Turns out they had received prestigious Fulbright scholarships and were headed off to Turkey, and as a result, they needed to sell their cupcake bakery — quickly.

It seemed like a heaven-sent opportunity! Here I was, baking up a storm, taking classes in baking science, researching bakeries — basically going whole hog in learning the ins and outs of my projected new profession. I had even taken a holiday job working in a local bakery, where I frosted over five hundred cookies a day. And now the very same people who had inspired my new passion were offering me the bakery that had started it all — and at a very fair price, I might add. I was over the moon!

I wanted us to buy that cupcakery so badly that I could taste it as if it were an actual cupcake. In fact, I could think of nothing else but taking over that bakery. There were a couple of problems, though, that my brain seemed to be unable — or unwilling — to register. Number one: My husband didn't want to move to Chicago, even though he was on board with the overall cupcakery idea. Number two: Although the asking price was eminently fair, buying any established business costs money — and I didn't have any.

After awhile I had to give up on the dream of owning the Chicago bakery, but I didn't give up on the *overall* dream. I decided that I would take my passion for a cupcakery and figure out how to make it work back home in New England. I knew that I needed to keep learning about baking, but I also needed to learn how to buy a business or start one with no money — and that meant figuring out a key component: business planning.

Now, I'm a planner by nature, anyway. Always have been, always will be. I enjoy dreaming up concepts and filling in all the details to make them work. I love developing ideas and going over and over them, watching them grow and expand into something real. Not surprisingly, I dove into the world of business planning like everything else I do: feetfirst for all I'm worth. I signed up for classes at my local Small Business

Administration office, I applied for a SCORE mentor (more on SCORE mentors later), and I bought every book on starting a business that our local bookstore had in stock, plus all the ones I could find online. Eric was equally invested. Together, we traveled to our chosen area of Massachusetts and looked at rental spaces. We studied up on health codes and requirements and met with a counselor to work on our small-business plan. We had appointments with credit experts and banks. We even chose a name for the cupcakery. Eric and I were beyond excited — even though something didn't feel right. Nonetheless, we forged ahead. . . .

I'll be honest with you about my first attempt at writing a business plan: it was easier to make a perfect batch of cupcakes with professional-looking frosting than it was to write that first draft of a professional-looking business plan. I found myself more interested in designing my very own cupcakery space and thinking about the perfect logo for my business than I was about projected revenues and figuring out the interest on a bank loan.

Truthfully, I was having a hard time understanding what I was trying so hard to learn. Most of the resources I had access to seemed like they were written in a foreign language. I found it tough to understand a lot of the words, let alone the meanings behind them.

I wasn't sure what I was *reading*, let alone what I was *writing*, but eventually I got it done. But even though I found it hard to digest all the reading I was doing, I managed to complete a business plan that we could literally take to the bank.

These days, I wouldn't use a lot of those same resources I used back then to write a business plan. Not only has the kind of business I own changed, but also — and luckily — the landscape of owning a business has changed from just a decade or so ago. But even though those old resources I used way back when wouldn't be useful to the business I have now, I did take something wonderful (and perhaps rather ironic) away from that first business-plan experience: I did *not want* to open my own cupcakery.

That's right. Putting together a business plan showed me that owning a bakery, of any kind, wasn't the right business for me to be in. I learned that I didn't want to work seven days a week. Plus, Eric and I were not comfortable taking out the sizable loan we would need to open a bakery from scratch and all that it

would entail. We decided that the amount of work the business would involve would just be too much. We suddenly realized that while we may be entrepreneurs at heart, owning a cupcakery was not the right fit for us. And that realization might not have come — or might have come at a hefty price tag — had I not developed a business plan.

My business plan helped me to learn not only what kind of business I *didn't* want to have but also a lot about what my personal values are. Turns out I value freedom *a lot*, and I wouldn't have that freedom if I was beholden to a schedule of store hours. The bottom line is that I learned what I did and did not want from a business where I was going to be the boss. And until I had that long, detailed bundle of facts and figures outlining in great, great detail what could be my future life, I had no idea that this seemingly perfect dream that I had been focused on for almost a year wasn't perfect at all.

Thank goodness for business plans.

ENTREPRENEURIAL BUSINESS PLANNING

When I traveled the United States promoting my first book, *The Handmade Marketplace: How to Sell Your Crafts Locally, Globally, and Online*, I had the pleasure and the privilege to meet a whole lot of people. People like me and probably people like you, too. Which is to say, creative people who love what they're doing but who need some extra help when it comes to running their businesses.

And if you think that as a creative entrepreneur, you're not in business in the traditional sense, and therefore things like business plans don't apply — well, think again. This book is for creative-business owners of all sorts. Whether you're a fabric designer or a graphic designer or a jewelry maker or a ukulele player, if you own or want to own a business based on your creative energy and ideas, you need to have a plan. True, our needs aren't always the same as folks who want to open other kinds of businesses like restaurants, day-care centers, or teeth-whitening boutiques, although owners of those businesses would find some value here, too. But the bottom line is the bottom line — and a business is a business, no matter what form it may take. You could be working in your basement or in your dining room. Maybe you're lucky enough to have a home studio, or you're working out of a dedicated bedroom, den, or even a closet. If you're thinking about growing bigger or expanding your efforts, it's time to make a plan.

From spending time with so many creative-business owners and reading lots of mail from people who took *The Handmade Marketplace* to heart, I've learned that when it comes to the next step in our enterprises, we're collectively looking for a new kind of business planning. We want to structure our lives and businesses in a way that makes sense to us. Since most of us run our businesses ourselves, sometimes with help from our families or with a partner, our business-planning needs are different from those of people who want to own more traditional companies.

Most of us won't need to take bank loans for large amounts of money to start our dream company or need to assemble a board of directors (in the traditional manner; more on this later) to steer us to success. A lot of us won't even need to rent a space of any kind, much less lease a suite of offices in a high-rise, to get our work done.

For the creative entrepreneur and the handmaker, our business-planning needs are different. There are lots of reasons for this, but it pretty much boils down to a basic fact: our values are a bit different.

Most of us want to run our business on our own terms. While it's possible that some of you are looking to rent the penthouse suite of the tallest building in town to run a creative empire from, I think most of you would be happy with a good workable space, essential equipment, health insurance, maybe some help on the side, and a steady paycheck that covers your bills and allows you to save for a cushy retirement.

Sure, we may need to borrow money for a computer upgrade or perhaps to do repairs on our vintage letterpress or to take a design class that keeps our skills sharp. And we may need to fund trips to craft shows that can boost our bottom line or to hire someone to help us with our marketing plans or design custom packaging. But this type of expense is exactly why we need a different kind of business plan, one that reflects the businesses we create and run — a plan that reflects our core personal values and our core business philosophies.

Lots of people shy away from planning. Many of my clients cite reasons like "I have a fear of commitment," or "planning would lock me into the unknown," and the ever-popular, "things change so fast, why bother planning?" I'm here to tell you that planning for your business and planning for your success isn't a burden. Planning doesn't mean that you won't have flexibility or the freedom to change your mind. In fact, it can be very liberating.

Chances are if you're reading this book, you already have a business of some sort. You could be selling your handmade goods at craft fairs or taking graphic design clients on the side while you work full-time for someone else. No matter what your enterprise looks like right now, if you're selling something you make or you perform a service, you have a business. Congratulations! And no matter where your business is in the grand scheme of your dream, you could use a business plan.

USING THIS BOOK

First things first: Keep a journal handy. This book is full of lots of prompts, called Exercises, and to make full use of them and to make the most out of our time together, I advise you to keep all of your answers, lists, and ideas in one convenient place.

It is my personal hope that you'll find this book useful, challenging, and as valuable a resource to you personally as your products and services are to your community. My intentions for *Grow Your Handmade Business* are to help you set goals, define your personal success, dream up plans that take your company where you want it to be *while* you take care of yourself, and make sure that your business life doesn't become all there is to your actual life.

So let's dig in and get started! I am thrilled to begin this exciting journey with you, and I hope that by our journey's end, you will have a plan in place that helps you to run the kind of creative business — and life — you have been dreaming about. Remember, I'm dreaming right along with you.

XO, Kari

MEET THE CREATIVE COLLECTIVE

Joining us on this journey are some really amazing entrepreneurs. This exceptional, eclectic group includes a copywriter, business strategists, crafters/handmakers, career and life coaches, a teacher, painters, and illustrators. They have graciously shared their struggles and successes, their top business-planning tips, and their best pieces of advice. I chose these folks because not only do I know them, I also know that what they have to offer is invaluable. It's an incredible opportunity for us to learn from some of the best and the brightest. Even if someone runs a different kind of business than yours, you can still learn from them. They have all been incredibly generous with their time and resources, and I'm forever grateful to all of them. You'll find a list of their websites in the back of the book, so please check them out and introduce yourself. Let them know Kari from *Grow Your Handmade Business* sent you!

ABBY KERR
Writer, *Abby Kerr Ink*
www.abbykerrink.com

Abby is a writer and a brand voice ally for indie online entrepreneurs who want to own their voices in the marketplace. Abby is a former national award-winning indie-lifestyle retailer and now runs her business successfully online. There is pretty much nothing Abby can't do. She is smart and friendly and one of my very best discoveries from my Twitter community.

ALEXANDRA FRANZEN
Writer
www.alexandrafranzen.com

A promotional writer with a keen eye for words that woo, Alexandra Franzen helps righteous entrepreneurs break their own sound barriers, with Whoa Nelly web copy, sales-page sorcery, and spooky-perfect ghostwriting. And better hair. I wanted to include Alex in this book because I've worked with her personally; she's helped me out of many a writing jam, particularly when it came to writing my own biography. She is a word machine and is supersweet to boot.

ALISON LEE
Designer/Podcaster, *CRAFTCAST*
www.craftcast.com

After spending 25 years laboring in the New York City ad-agency trenches, Alison Lee set off on a new adventure. She created *CRAFTCAST*, a podcast dedicated to all things craft related. She also hosts popular live online craft classes. Teachers and students from around the world log on to learn new skills from Alison and the expert instructors in these 90-minute sessions. I have spent many a "crafternoon" listening to Alison's podcast. Her guests are always fascinating and the topics she covers are always useful. If you haven't downloaded and listened to all episodes of *CRAFTCAST*, get thee to your computer and start listening!

BETTIE NEWELL
Business Lawyer / Photographer / Community Leader
www.littlepapercities.com
www.tonkon.com

Bettie is one of my tip-top favorite business ladies. She successfully scaled back her full-time career to follow her creative dreams. While she still practices law, she also has a fledgling photography business originating from her true creative love: her camera. She lives and works in Portland, Oregon.

DEB THOMPSON
Gallery Owner,
Nahcotta / Enormous Tiny Art
www.nahcotta.com
www.enormoustinyart.com

Deb Thompson opened Nahcotta in May 2000 in Portsmouth, New Hampshire. She subsequently launched the Enormous Tiny Art Shows in 2007, which are held twice a year (and always online) at Nahcotta to provide accessible, original art to her clients. Nahcotta features rotating exhibitions of contemporary art, gifts, and furniture from independent artists and designers. I make the eight-hour round-trip drive to Deb's gallery whenever I can. The space is beautiful, and the products she sells, as well as the art she shows and sells, are always top-notch. If I had a brick-and-mortar business, I'd model it after Nahcotta. It's wonderful!

HEATHER BAILEY
Designer
www.heatherbailey.typepad.com

Heather Bailey is one of the most creative women I know of. She has run several successful businesses, creating everything from children's hats to hair ties. Heather's designs have been featured in numerous magazines, including *InStyle*, *Glamour*, *Mademoiselle*, *Seventeen*, and *Country Living*, and her amazing artwork can be found on products ranging from paper napkins to, of course, fabric.

JAY MCCARROLL
Fashion Designer / Fabric Designer,
www.jaymccarrollonline.com

Jay is famous for winning season 1 of *Project Runway*. As far back as Jay can recall, he has been drawn to textiles. One of his oldest memories includes a satin-trimmed, blue-fleece blanket that he lovingly called his "feeling thing." Jay recently formed several corporations for the purpose of expanding the reach of Jay McCarroll designs and brands. He launched his online shop, Jay McCarroll Online, and is focusing on providing fun and exciting new merchandise to his fans and customers.

JENA CORAY
Professional Blogger / Publicity Maven / Trend Forecaster, *Miss Modish*
www.missmodish.com
www.modishblog.com

The serial entrepreneur and marketing mistress behind Miss Modish, Jena Coray, offers inspired consulting, marketing, and PR services to artists, handmakers, and indie-preneurs who are interested in taking their businesses to the next level of awesome! I am not even sure when I first became aware of Jena. It seems like Miss Modish has always been a part of my personal creative online life. We met for the first time while I was on tour for *The Handmade Marketplace*, and I knew right away that I had met a kindred spirit.

JENNIFER LEE
Author/Coach, *Artizen Coaching*
www.artizencoaching.com
www.rightbrainbusinessplan.com

The founder of Artizen Coaching and author of *The Right-Brain Business Plan*, Jennifer Lee spent a decade climbing the corporate ladder before pursuing her creative dreams. Through her popular workshops, coaching practice, and writing, she encourages and empowers others to follow their passions. I adore Jennifer Lee. She is creative, kind, and full of good ideas and is one of my first stops when I need a creative pick-me-up.

JESSICA SWIFT
Artist/Designer
www.jessicaswift.com

Jessica Swift, a full-time, independent artist and surface pattern designer in Atlanta, Georgia, has big dreams! From licensed artwork used on others' products (one example: iPhone covers) to objects made in her own home studio, Jessica's eponymous brand of surface design and vibrant gift / home products is centered on her daring use of color and her quirky and fun pattern sense. Jess is as colorful as her artwork. Spending time on her website, or with her on the phone, is time well spent. She is like a human battery recharger, and I'm so glad to know her.

JESSIE OLESON
Author / Artist / Store Owner, *CakeSpy*
www.cakespy.com

Writer, illustrator, gallery owner, and cake anthropologist Jessie Oleson runs CakeSpy, an award-winning website dedicated to seeking out the sweet things in life. She calls it a Dessert Detective Agency. Jessie is also the author of *CakeSpy Presents: Sweet Treats for a Sugar-Filled Life*, a book of recipes and illustrations. When in Seattle, be sure to check out her new retail gallery, CakeSpy Shop. Jessie is one of my most favorite people ever.

JOLIE GUILLEBEAU
Painter/Artist
www.jolieguillebeau.com

Jolie Guillebeau is a storyteller and painter in Portland, Oregon. She believes in creating something every single day, to-do lists written in orange pen, and hand-knit socks. She is incapable of answering a question with a single-word answer or declining dessert. Jolie and I "met" many years ago in an online course to help people actualize their dreams. Since that course, I've followed Jolie online, and I think she's amazing. Check out her daily paintings on her website.

KARIE SUTHERLAND

Professional Organizer / Event Planner, *Order Ahead*
www.orderaheadorganizing.com

A professional organizer in the Chicago area (her motto is "Leave Your Organizing Obstacles Behind!"), Karie Sutherland helps the creative with their business organizing needs, including event and office/studio space organization. Full disclosure: Karie is not only a professional organizer, she is also my very closest friend. I can vouch for her professional skills though, because right before I began writing this book, she flew out to my home to help me get my office in tip-top shape so I could focus on my book instead of on my mess.

KELLY RAE ROBERTS

Author/Artist
www.kellyraeroberts.com

Artist and author Kelly Rae Roberts describes herself as a "possibilitarian." Since discovering her passion for painting, Kelly Rae has built a broad online following, written a best-selling book, been featured in multiple publications, mentored thousands of artists through her popular blog and e-courses, and launched wildly successful gift and home-decor collections through her licensing deals. Having spent most of her life in the company of women, her pieces grow out of the kindred support she has felt from many of them throughout her life.

KRISTEN RASK

Author / Designer / Store Owner, *Schmancy Toys*
www.schmancytoys.com

With a mission to provide quirky toys, collectibles, and original artwork to the world, Kristen Rask opened her toy store, Schmancy, in downtown Seattle in September 2004. Kristen is also the founder and curator of Plush You, an annual exhibit that showcases plush creations from artists all over the globe. Since then, Plush You has grown tremendously, with a book released from F+W Publications in 2007 and an enormous list of yearly applicants ensuring that Plush You continues to show the world the impressive and boundless possibilities of plush!

LISA CONGDON
Artist/Illustrator,
Lisa Congdon Art & Illustration
www.lisacongdon.com

Lisa Congdon is a San Francisco–based illustrator and fine artist. Raised in both upstate New York and Northern California, Lisa grew up loving the trees and animals that surrounded her — a love that is now expressed in her colorful paintings and drawings. Her clients include Chronicle Books, Running Press, HarperCollins Publishers, Target, Pottery Barn Teen, Urban Outfitters, and Land of Nod. She is the author of *A Collection a Day*, which was spawned from a 2010 creative endeavor.

MEGAN AUMAN
Designer/Educator,
Designing an MBA
http://designinganmba.com

Megan Auman is a designer, handmaker, and educator who built a multifaceted business around her passion for great design and sustainable business. Her eponymous jewelry line is sold in stores across the United States and online. She also founded Designing an MBA to help designers and artisans develop their business skills. Bookmark her website to keep up to date with all the great advice she shares with her community.

MEGAN HUNT
Designer, *Princess Lasertron*
www.princesslasertron.com
www.campcoworking.com

Megan Hunt lives in Omaha, Nebraska, where she devotes much of her time to supporting local entrepreneurs and creatives through her coworking space, CAMP. She works through the night making floral accessories for brides, designing dresses for fabulous people, and sharing inspiration with her customers through her website. What she loves most about her job is meeting and collaborating with passionate dreamers; speaking in front of great big crowds; and being able to take her daughter, Alice, to work every day. Megan's passion for creative business ventures is evident. She is motivation in motion.

MICHAEL ELLIOTT
Certified Public Accountant,
Michael Elliott, CPA
www.geaugacpa.com

CPA extraordinaire Michael Elliott loves helping creative people because they, too, are innovative and interested in utilizing the newest tools and technologies possible to help grow their businesses. When I put a call out on Twitter asking people to send info on a funny, kind accounting person who had experience working with small creative-business owners, his name was sent to me. After a few conversations, I knew he was the right numbers-advice person for this book. I think you're going to love his interview!

MICHELLE WARD
Creative Career Coach,
When I Grow Up Coach
www.whenigrowupcoach.com

Michelle Ward, a.k.a. the When I Grow Up Coach, helps creative people devise the career they think they can't have — or discover it to begin with! A life coach certified by the International Coach Academy, a musical-theater actress with a BFA from NYU/Tisch School of the Arts, and a Corporate America escapee, Michelle has served as an expert source and contributor for such mainstream outlets as *Newsweek*, *Forbes*, and *Psychology Today* while still getting away with saying "amaze-balls" a heck of a lot.

NICOLE BALCH
Designer / Professional Blogger,
Making It Lovely / Pink Loves Brown
www.makingitlovely.com

Nicole Balch is a designer living outside of Chicago. I first became aware of Nicole many years ago, when I fell in love with her stationery designs. Now the world turns to her website to get the latest on home-design trends. Her blog, *Making it Lovely*, was named one of the "50 World's Best Design Blogs" by the *London Times Online*. Her work has been featured in *Better Homes & Gardens*, *The Chicago Tribune Magazine*, *Time Out Chicago*, *ReadyMade*, and *Everyday with Rachael Ray*, among other publications. She is a great example of someone who took her passion and branched out in different directions.

REBECCA PEARCY

Designer / Awesome Lady,
Queen Bee Creations / Chickpea Baby / Rebecca Pearcy Textiles
www.queenbee-creations.com
www.chickpeababy.com
www.rebeccapearcy.com

Rebecca Pearcy founded Queen Bee Creations in 1996 from a corner in her bedroom. Now Rebecca and her team of skilled worker bees design and hand make their bags, wallets, and accessories at their studio in Portland, Oregon. Rebecca has since added a line of diaper bags with Chickpea Baby, and most recently a line of original and sustainable textile prints for home and life with Rebecca Pearcy Textiles. Some of you may remember my Queen Bee story from *The Handmade Marketplace.* It was one of the very first crafty businesses I discovered online, and I've been a loyal customer ever since.

SUE EGGEN

Designer, *Giant Dwarf*
www.giantdwarfdesign.com

Sue Eggen is an incredible designer, and I've been a customer of hers for years. She is clever and creative and makes the most amazing hats and accessories. She lives in South Philly, but her design inventiveness is available around the globe via her website and Etsy store. Her photographs are lovely, and you can learn a lot from her by simply studying her online presence.

TARA GENTILE

Coach / Teacher / Inspiration Leader,
Tara Gentile / Scoutie Girl
www.taragentile.com
www.scoutiegirl.com

Tara Gentile is an online business professional who helps people define their ideas by looking deeper into what they really want to create. She is also the author of several online business courses and e-books, including *The Art of Earning* and *Making Motion: 7 Steps for Doing More with Your Creative Life.* Tara is one of the very best business resources I know of. On her website and in her online resources like e-books and courses, she writes passionately about everything from finding your muse to how to feel good about earning what you deserve. Tara is a treasure.

Part 1

MAPPING
YOUR DREAM

Chapter 1

IDENTIFY YOUR DREAM BUSINESS

Dreaming big is one of the best (not to mention the most affordable!) business skills you have. Being successful doesn't mean that you have all the answers and you have nothing left to work for. If you play your cards right, your dreams will always be growing and expanding. Realizing a dream is definitely an aspiration — but first you need to actually identify your dream.

WHAT FORM DOES YOUR DREAM BUSINESS TAKE?

Exactly what does the ideal dream business look like to you? Surely you've thought about it . . . right? Perhaps you've deemed that business as too far-fetched to be even remotely possible. Or perhaps that ideal couldn't possibly be so perfect because it doesn't match up with what most people would consider an ideal business. Well, friend, I'm here to tell you otherwise.

Your ideal business or even the business you have now doesn't have to look like someone else's business. Your perfect business may simply be one that lets you keep your full-time job. Or your perfect business may be you sitting behind a big desk with lots of employees that keep things running while you focus on designing products. Sitting down and taking stock of what you really want to accomplish will get you headed in the right direction. Dreaming big is a key component of the process.

Imagining the life of someone you admire is a great way to get your dream juices flowing, but think really carefully about what you're envisioning. For example, Martha Stewart's life looks great, right? She has lots of amazing houses and lovely animals and everything always seems perfect, plus she has her own media empire. She's world famous, can bake a perfect turkey for Thanksgiving, can whip up clever party favors in seconds flat, and even has a gift-wrapping center in her home. Sounds awfully good!

And it may well be. But she is also responsible for employing an army of people. She works tons of hours. She has to be "on" and perfect all the time (can you imagine that every time you ate dinner out, it made the papers?!). And, well, *she's Martha Stewart*! That's a lot of pressure to be under, I would imagine.

Clearly, there are both an upside and a downside to her business life. Does the downside sound just as good to you as the rest? If so, super! If not, that's OK. Frankly, it doesn't sound all that great to me, either. I like weekends to myself and being able to wear my yoga pants to the grocery store once in a while without fear of having my photograph end up on the "Fashion Faux Pas" page of a gossip magazine.

But that's the beauty of having your own business. It can look however you want it to look, and it can be whatever you want it to be. Let's face it though; it's not always easy to know exactly what you want, and when you're forming your overall picture of perfect business bliss, it's really important to be completely honest with yourself.

Here are some questions to ask when trying to decide what your perfect business life would look like:

- How many hours weekly do you *want* to work on your business?
- How many hours weekly can you *actually* work on your business?
- Where will you do this work?

FROM THE CREATIVE COLLECTIVE: MEGAN HUNT

I started Princess Lasertron when I was 19, and when I was 23, I founded CAMP, a coworking space where I share my studio with about a dozen other local small businesses. As I look back through my life and think about who I am and what I believe, I can see that following my passion to become a creative entrepreneur was the "natural" path for me. I was born to do this. I'm impulsive, decisive, resourceful; I tend to have an alpha-type personality; and I've been making stuff throughout my entire childhood and adulthood. From the time I was in high school, I never saw myself being happy in a corporate job or sitting behind a desk, so I never prepared for that kind of life. I put in the work early to become my own boss, and I've never known anything else in my working life.

- How much money will this business need to get off the ground/grow?

- How much money do you have to actually contribute to this business?

- Do you have all the tools that you need to make this business successful?

- What systems do you already have in place that can help make this business successful?

- What makes THIS your dream business?

- If you were applying for a job at your own business, what qualities and qualifications do you possess that make you a good match for what this business needs?

- Do you have any weak spots in your skill set? How can you work on them?

- What makes you deliriously, over-the-moon happy when you envision your business life?

- Do you see yourself being able to personally grow as your business grows? Will it offer you challenges that are a good match for your personality and working style?

- Speaking of working style, do you know what yours is?

- Do you have professional and personal support — people whom you can talk things through with or lean on if you have a problem?

- Have you ever worked for yourself before? All by yourself? What did you like about it? Did you find anything especially difficult?

- What motivates you? What really gets you going?

- If you didn't make this business happen successfully, how would you feel?

- And last, but perhaps most important, how would you feel if you didn't even try?

FROM THE CREATIVE COLLECTIVE: JENA CORAY

Focus on your specialness and how you're different from all your competitors. Don't seek to fit in or cash in on trends or be similar to anything you've ever seen before. Be different. Be brave. Follow your truth, and you'll find the people who want to listen — trust in that.

It's important to be impeccably honest with yourself here. For example, regarding a time commitment, you may think that you can work 15 hours a week on your business, but if you're already working 35 or 40 hours full-time somewhere else and/or have other responsibilities outside of your business — like community commitments, a family, or even just errands that need to be run or a dog that needs a long walk every day — then perhaps 15 hours is too much. Really, we all need our beauty sleep!

FROM THE CREATIVE COLLECTIVE: **TARA GENTILE**

When I went full-time with my business, I thought I would be this amazing ball of productivity. Eight hours?! I could accomplish anything in eight hours! And I'm sure I could . . . but I don't. I don't accomplish that much more in eight hours than I do in three or four. So I constrain my time and work less instead of procrastinating more.

Pennsylvania-born fashion designer Jay McCarroll gained fame after winning the first season of Project Runway, *the TV fashion-competition reality show. He shares some of his thoughts about being in business for yourself.*

ON NAMING YOUR BUSINESS

Think very carefully before you decide on the name for your business. If you go the eponymous route, calling the business after yourself, your name becomes the brand. Be sure you're willing to face any and all ramifications of having your name associated with your business for all time. It's hard to change your mind once you've reached some success.

ON BEING WIRED FOR BUSINESS

If you come from a family of business owners, as I do (my father owned a successful concrete business), don't feel that you should already know everything about running your own company. Everyone has a different learning curve, and you can set your own standards for your rate of both learning and success.

ON STRUCTURING YOUR BUSINESS

The infrastructure of your business is very important. Take a good, hard look at the way you have things set up, and don't be afraid to make adjustments if you need to.

ON MULTIPLE INCOME STREAMS

If you have more than one income stream, chances are you're busier than you would be if you only had one focus. Pay attention to every opportunity you choose to follow, taking careful note of what is truly rewarding to you and what may be wasting your valuable time.

ON PROTECTING YOUR BRAND

Make sure you are the owner of your business ID, like your website's domain name and all of your trademarks. Keep careful track of all of your records pertaining to these areas of your business. When you give your passwords out to designers or other people who may need them, change them to a default one first, and then change your password again when their work is done.

ON BEING PASSIONATE ABOUT YOUR BUSINESS

You can be passionate about a lot of things without needing them to be your main source of income. Hold a few things you love to do in abeyance, and do them when you're feeling a creative lull. I love to play around with color — I can lose myself for hours experimenting with different color combinations. Having a few creative tricks tucked up your sleeve is a great way to beat the dreaded creativity block.

A LAST WORD OF ADVICE

Stick with what you know best, and hire out for the rest!

WHAT DIRECTION(S) WILL YOUR DREAM BUSINESS TAKE?

When you're dreaming up your dreamy dream business, you need to be clear about just what exactly you want to do. This is not to say that your business can't have many different arms and components to it; this just means that you need to be very, very clear about the skills you bring to the table and just what it is that you want to do with them.

If, say, you're a graphic designer, do you want to mostly make collateral materials for people? Do you want to work with a coding professional and create websites? Would you like to focus on designing packaging for yarn companies? Do you want to design stationery? Or would you rather design signs for hip restaurants in your town? Do you dream of seeing your invitation in wedding magazines? Or would you most like to work with bands to create their album artwork and concert posters?

You get the idea. A graphic designer can go in many different directions. One main skill, awesome designing ability, can be used in so many exciting places.

Deciding on a direction is important because your business needs a home base of sorts. You need a center, a place to return to when you're overworked or confused, need to scale back, or want to build out and expand. As a creative-business owner, who are you at the core? What is it exactly that you do? Get out your journal, and finish these sentences:

➤➤ My strongest creative skill is

_____

➤➤ My favorite thing to sell is

_____

_____

➤➤ My most popular product is

_____

_____

➤➤ People most ask me for

_____

_____

➤➤ When I look at the list of things I need to do for a normal day-in-the-life of my business, the thing I want to do the most is

_____

_____

- My weakest skill that I use is
  _____
  _____

- My least favorite project or product for my business is
  _____
  _____

- I love to do it, but I hardly ever sell
  _____
  _____

- If I never had to _____
  for my business, it would be too soon.

OK, now look at what you've written. What do your answers have in common with one another? Do you notice a pattern in your answers? How do you feel about them? Perhaps your answers look something like:

- *Writing*

- *Zines*

- *Monthly vegan zine*

- *Copywriting help*

- *Write/cook*

- *Photography*

- *Business cards*

- *Custom-designed recipe cards*

- *Use most forms of social media*

With these answers, you will have discovered a lot about yourself in just the few minutes it took to respond to the questions. You like to write and cook, but you feel weak when it comes to photography. You can make and design printed materials, like zines and business cards and probably lots of other things. You make some money doing copywriting, but writing for hire doesn't show up anywhere else on your list.

So this Q&A session has given you a better understanding of how and where to begin building your business foundation. You now know that as you explore the nooks and crannies of business planning and development, writing will (or should!) play a strong role, and that gives you a great place to start.

Of course, questions like these aren't the only way — or maybe even the best way — for you to figure out what your foundation is. Perhaps you already know what you're exceptional at and where your skill set lies. If so, good for you! Either way, once you have some solid ideas about what it is you want to do, you need to start thinking about where you want to go with your talents. And before you can truly figure out the nuts and bolts of your amazing enterprise, whether you have a business now or you bought this book because you want to build one, you first have to know yourself.

Right about now you may be saying to yourself, *Wait a second. Am I starting/expanding a business, or going into therapy*?! Well, the fact of the matter is, the success of your business depends on you, and you are human. You have strengths, shortcomings, superpowers, and areas where you might want to improve. Both your personal life and your business life are comprised of the choices you make, and you can make better, stronger choices if you get really clear on where you are and where you want to go. There are no right or wrong answers. There are just choices that will change how you operate. You can always rework your choices, and you can always change your mind. That is the true beauty of being the boss and of being who you really want to be.

Over time, your answer to the next question may change, but take stock of where you are right now, at this exact point in your business: *What would make you the happiest*?

Everything is changing so fast right now. Growing up, I couldn't have imagined that the work I do now would even exist! Staying flexible and open to new opportunities will serve one well. I constantly review where I am and where I want to be. I'm always thinking ahead about the next step I need to take and how I can continue to grow my business.

Chapter 2

DREAM BUSINESS FUNDAMENTALS

Businesses come in all shapes and sizes. Deciding to dive in fully committed to your business is a way to tell if what you have is a sometimes-profitable hobby or if your future lies in a full-fledged business.

DO YOU HAVE A HOBBY OR A BUSINESS?

What's the difference between a hobby and a business? Well, to my way of thinking, a hobby is something you do because you love it and expect nothing back other than personal satisfaction. If you make a profit on it here and there, or even sell something and just recoup your costs, it's still a hobby. You love doing it, and it's nice to make a little cash on the side.

A business, on the other hand, is something you do for profit. Fortunately these days, with our new economy and our huge creative community, you can also run a business for love as well as profit (lucky us!). Running a business means that you are selling something (products or services) to make money. Your objectives are to support yourself, meet your financial goals, and be your own boss.

But to create a booming business, you'll need more than just creativity or a genius idea or loads of cash in the bank. You'll need other skills and abilities. You must simultaneously be a boss, a manager, a bookkeeper, a designer, a salesperson, a marketing director, a public relations person, and a budgeting wiz, among other talents. In fact, you're about to wear so many

FROM THE CREATIVE COLLECTIVE: KRISTEN RASK

The only way to know if you should start your own business is to try. It's a huge risk, but it can change your life in huge and amazing ways. Some people soon realize that they aren't businesspeople, and they can put that dream to rest. Other people may realize that they are more adept than they thought. You can go at your own pace to an extent, but you have to know that there will be hardships and pain along the way. Living the dream is really hard.

hats, you should consider building a walk-in closet to hold them all.

A HOBBY IS GREAT . . . AND SO IS A BUSINESS!

Getting back to the hobby-versus-business question, having a creative passion is a wonderful thing. Having a hobby where you also earn some money back for your time and investment is a great way to get your feet wet and see if you really want to or *could* turn your endeavor into a full-on business.

By all means, you could take things slow and just see how it goes. If you're not ready to jump in with both feet, there is no reason to do so. That's where business planning comes in. Working up a business plan will help you to see the directions you could take if you choose to do so, and it can help you figure out exactly what it is you're working toward.

There is nothing wrong with having a hobby that brings you much joy,

HOBBY OR BUSINESS? THE TAX MAN KNOWETH

In the United States, the Internal Revenue Service sees a distinct difference between a hobby and a business when it comes to paying taxes. How and what you claim comes into play, and your bookkeeper or accountant can help you with that.

Even a hobby can benefit from a business plan. If your aim is to *someday* turn that hobby into a business, planning to do so is the right place to start.

If you're still in the happy-hobby stage, start small. Keep track of how long finishing a project takes. Record the money you spend on that project from beginning to end. While you're working on it, notice how you feel. Could you do this over and over, all day, every day? Do you have ideas about how you would market or sell what you're making?

This is basic research, and if you decide to turn what you're doing into a legitimate business, these kinds of project notes will come in handy.

offers you an outlet for your creative expression, and makes you feel good. It doesn't have to go beyond that . . . unless you really, *really* want it to.

WHERE ARE YOU NOW, AND WHERE ARE YOU GOING?

Chances are, you'll be able to relate to at least one of these scenarios:

I have no idea where I want to go because I'm not sure what my choices might be. You love to crochet, and you're good at it. The few craft fairs you've hawked your wares at have sold out. You're able to take custom requests from local folks, and you just created a website so that you can expand your sales potential. Recently a local yarn store asked if you'd like to teach classes, and people have begun to ask you for copies of your original patterns. When you step back and look at your big picture, it seems like you have many opportunities, but you don't have any idea what you *really* want to do or what you should focus on. All you know is that you want to turn all of these amazing chances into something profitable, but you know you can't do everything at once.

I want to grow my business. You've been plugging away and chugging along at the same pace for a while now. You've identified areas

---

FROM THE CREATIVE COLLECTIVE: ALISON LEE

For me a hobby turned into a business. As I got more serious about my website CRAFTCAST, I realized I had to respect it as a business for it to grow. A business plan can change, but having one removes some daily stress and is the vision that supports making your dreams and plans a reality.

RUNNING MY OWN BUSINESS...

"Running my own business has grown me up from the 'adolescence' of my adulthood into full-fledged adulthood, which is still expanding and evolving. It's allowed me to claim who I am and how I want to experience my life in the world."
— ABBY KERR

"Running my own business means I'm happier. I enjoy getting up and getting to work. I even love all the parts of business ownership that I may have scoffed at years ago — like bookkeeping, self-promotion, even packing and shipping. I've learned so much about what I am capable of that I never would have known [had I not gone into business for myself]."
— LISA CONGDON

of your business that would be easy to expand, and you're up for the challenge. You're pleased with your customer base and most details of your enterprise. Your prices are good, and you're bringing in enough money to take some risks. Your nuts and bolts are mostly in place, and you are more than ready to begin a new adventure.

I want my business to stay the same but be better organized. You are happy with everything you're doing for the most part. While you love your product lines, and the response from the public is good, and the money you net makes you happy, you are feeling overwhelmed. You may have trouble shipping out your goods when you're scheduled to do so, and your studio is a mess because you don't even have the time or energy to sort out the chaos. You haven't seen your bookkeeper in months, and you're facing a big tax payment. Often, to finish up a project, you have to place an online order or run out for supplies. You know you're on the right track; you just have trouble *staying* on track.

Running your own business is not for everyone. When I was fifteen, I wanted to be a dancer. I had a wonderful teacher who said, "You dance because you have to, not because you want to." The same holds true in having your own business.

I want to divest some of my business responsibilities so I can have tighter focus. Your company grew so fast! Before you knew it, your little sewing enterprise turned into a real business. You have local stores calling for products, and they need help with displays. Your online store is more empty than full because your products sell so quickly. You're thinking about seeking out a manufacturing option, but you don't have time to do the necessary research. You dream of getting back to doing what you love best: designing children's clothing. But your brain is too scattered, and the last thing you seem to have time for is what got you started in this venture to begin with.

EXERCISE
Try writing your own example about yourself and your business. Where are you at? What are your biggest concerns? What do you want to improve the most?

ONWARD AND UPWARD

No matter where you are right now, together we're going to get you to where you want to be. We're going to first examine the various directions in which you can take your company, and then break down the different components of a business plan. We'll help you to devise a strategy that will get you on track and keep you on that track — the fast track to getting what you want out of your business.

OK, let's get started!

Chapter 3

WORKING FOR YOUR VISION

Starting a business or pumping up the volume on an already-operating venture is hard work. Trust me when I tell you that you'll never work harder days than the ones you work for yourself. Being your own boss is tough, and running a company while running your life can be tricky.

If you decide to do it, though, it'll be one of the best times of your life, including those exhausting days. Being fully in charge of your destiny and your future is an amazing feeling. The sense of freedom, doing what you love, and feeling accomplished goes a long way and will sustain you on even the toughest of days.

A BUSINESS TAKES WORK, AND PLENTY OF IT

It goes without saying that you need to be totally committed to what you're doing. Your business will demand 100 percent of whatever it is you have to give, and you have to meet it more than halfway. Being flexible is an absolute must. Sometimes things won't go your way, and sometimes the abundance of your efforts will stockpile up to the point where your head will spin.

Success doesn't usually come overnight, of course. (Wouldn't it be nice if it did?) But putting the time and effort in your business and going back to the drawing board again and again, and then again if need be, will take you far. Be ready for any possibility, my friend! With a little planning, that flexibility requirement, and a good support system, the sky's the limit. There is no end to what you can create, be, or do.

ACCEPT WHAT YOU DETEST . . . AND DO IT ANYWAY

We all have things we can't bear doing. For me, it's numbers. I would rather do just about anything than balance my books, organize my receipts, or invoice clients, not to mention try to project my estimated revenue for the next two financial quarters. The truth is, though, that my desire to make my dreams come true and build the best business I can is stronger than my fear and loathing of figuring out my bottom line.

There are workdays when all I want to do is curl up on my sofa with my dogs and a good book and read the day away. I can barely manage to get out of bed, let alone to my studio. Sometimes my crochet hook calls to me at very inopportune times, and

I feel the urge to put my business aside, wind all of my yarn, and work on an impromptu scarf design. I'm sure you can relate. Even if you don't work exclusively for yourself, days like these are possible when you go into your employer's place of business, too. You are supposed to be working on a report or straightening shelves, and you find yourself checking Facebook 20 times an hour.

You'll need to learn what triggers your desire to slack off. Do you dread what your tasks are for the day? Is your project not exciting? Does your loathing of what's on your agenda stem from your lack of expertise in the area of what you need to get done? Or, do you just plain old need a break because you aren't taking enough time for yourself?

When all is said and done, though, the one thing that will make your business a success is clear and simple: YOU. You must be willing to do the work. You have to get your butt into the desk chair or behind the potter's wheel or pick up your camera or whatever it is your creative dreams are made of. Being clear on what motivates you and what you really want will help you put those lazy I-don't-wanna days into perspective.

FROM THE CREATIVE COLLECTIVE: LISA CONGDON

If you are a maker, you usually just want to make stuff, so forcing yourself to sit down and do regular bookkeeping and office organization can be really challenging. It was for me, but then I set up a system in which I set aside half a day a week where I don't go to my studio. Instead, I stay home and do my books for the week, clean my office, answer emails, etc. Now I actually look forward to this time each week to clean my slate.

HAVING YOUR OWN BUSINESS CAN CHANGE YOUR LIFE!

Is all of this worth it? Let's be brutally honest here: Creating or maintaining a business is hard work! You'll have so much to do, and some of it won't be enjoyable. So really, is all that freedom-gaining, dream-following, making-your-own-decisions, working-for-yourself, being-your-happiest work self really worth it? You bet it is, friend! Don't just take my word for it, though; here's what busy business folks from the Creative Collective have to say about taking the plunge.

"Not that being a Woman of the World (what I call being a full-time entrepreneur) is a bed of roses all the time, but let's say this: It's 4 p.m. on a Monday, and I'm writing this on my laptop while sitting on a bench in the park on a sunny, 75-degree day in jeans, a T-shirt, and my hair in pigtails. It's not a bad life. As a bonus, [since starting my business] I've met more like-minded, creative, passionate, unique, amazeballs folks. I've seriously never felt so surrounded by so many people who share my mindset in one way or another."
— **MICHELLE WARD**

"I am free. I am full. I am voltaic. I am not surrounded by beige cubicle walls. I do not attend bland and rambling all-staff meetings. I do not set my alarm clock for 6:45 A.M. I do not spend 10 percent of my waking hours on a bus or commuter train. I work underneath a feather duvet. I adore my clients. I swim in the flow of love, ambition, and collaborative vision. I am happy. How profound!"
— **ALEXANDRA FRANZEN**

45

"I'd say some of the biggest changes since owning my own business have been in my freedom (being able to work from anywhere in the world, and being free to travel), confidence (knowing that I'm good at what I do and being able to make a living from it), and learning to be assertive (setting my own boundaries, especially around time and money)."
— JOLIE GUILLEBEAU

"I love being in charge of my own schedule and getting to travel when I want/need to. I never have to ask for time off work or save up vacation days or anything like that. I get to do what I want to do when I need to do it! It's also amazing to me to be in charge of my own success. Everything that I've achieved has been directly because of me, and that's an amazing feeling that I'd never trade to work for someone else."
— JESSICA SWIFT

"Running a business has empowered me, taught me lessons about myself, and shown me strengths that I didn't know I had. It's a blessing and a burden, really the best thing ever and the hardest thing ever, but I think that's what makes it so great. It's self-created, it's a manifestation of you, it's what you make of it. And the more passion and love and energy you put into your business, the more rewarding it will be, and that's pretty dang cool."
— JENA CORAY

"I feel I've accomplished a life-long goal of figuring out what I'd like to do with my life to keep me financially afloat while having fun plus being truly happy at the same time."
— SUE EGGEN

"I have so much less free time! It's enabled me to design exactly the life I want, though. Yes, I'm incredibly busy, especially since I've become a parent now, too, but I can structure my work in a way that fits into my life instead of living my life around a 9-to-5 job."
— NICOLE BALCH

RECHARGING

When you work for someone else, usually a part of your benefit package includes personal days. Don't be afraid to build some personal days into your own business structure. We all need to honor that day when we wake up hit with a big blast of spring fever. (At the very least, if you really, truly need a midafternoon nap, take one!) Sometimes your creative mind needs to recharge itself, and if you're ignoring the signals, your avoidance can just get worse.

VISUALIZE YOUR PERFECT WORKDAY

I'd like to teach you one of my favorite exercises. It's a visualization exercise, and I learned it from one of my virtual mentors, life coach Martha Beck. (More on mentors, virtual and otherwise, later.) I think Ms. Beck got it from someone else, but since I learned her way of doing it, it's the way I'm going to teach you. This exercise comes in really handy when you want to get a bit more clarity about what you really want. In fact, use it for your life in general as well as for your business! If you want to do it with me, you can go to my website, www.karichapin.com, and download an audio file that will walk you through it. But, honestly, it's not necessary to have the audio version for this to work.

It's best to do when you're in the planning and dreaming part of creating your business. I also like to do it when I feel like I've hit a wall or I'm having a problem that I just can't seem to solve. Simply read through these questions and keep them in your mind. Then, find a relaxing space and close your eyes and walk yourself though them. When you're done, reflect on your answers and pull out what seems to be the most important to you, and then think about those details more. When you're done, take note of what made you feel the best. What did you enjoy most about this day?

I want you to not only think of the answers to these questions, but also try to see them in your mind. Make a little movie in your brain and watch it play out as you see yourself answering these questions. There is no wrong way to do this, and if visualization isn't your thing, well, that's OK, too. You can skip ahead. But maybe you should give it a try just once.

Here we go....

VISUALIZATION EXERCISE

You are waking up in your home on a typical workday. There is nothing special about today except that it's in your future. It could be six months from now, next year, or five years from now. Your business is already established, and you're successful. Money is not a consideration, and you don't have any significant business worries in this scenario.

You wake up in your perfect bedroom in your perfect house. What does it look like? Notice the sheets on your bed, the color of your walls, what you're wearing. Take in everything about this perfect, wonderful place.

Get out of your bed and do what you normally do next. Do you go into your kitchen and start a pot of coffee or put the kettle on for tea? Or, do you head straight to the bathroom and hop in the shower? In your mind movie, just do whatever you normally do. Notice the details though, for example, what the rest of your house looks like and what you look like.

Continue on with your usual day in your mind. By now you've had breakfast, worked out, walked your dog, or gotten your kids off to school — visualize whatever you normally do.

MOVE ON TO PHASE TWO
In your perfect mind dream, where do you go to do your work? Do you go to your airy, spacious office located in the west wing of your mansion? Do you hop into your dream car and head to your chic office in a high-rise building? Do you go to your beautiful shop that's located

in an ideal location in your favorite neighborhood? Do you go to your workshop in a funky building in the industrial section of your town?

Once in your space, I want you to notice where it is and what it looks like. Drink in all the details of where you run your enterprise or your empire. Do you work at a desk equipped with a state-of-the-art computer system and printer? At a table covered with gorgeous fabric scraps? At a big easel splattered with paint with a big canvas perched on it? As you look around your space, what do you see? What do you do there?

Do clients come in and out all day? Do you have someone to answer the phone for you? Do you have customers? Do you see a packing and shipping area? Are the walls lined with shelves that are stocked with supplies? Do you see a workspace filled with sewing machines?

You can continue this exercise by envisioning the rest of your workday, or you can stop here.

TAKE STOCK

When you're done, take note of what you saw and how it made you feel.

Did you gain any clarity about yourself as a businessperson? Any clarity about your business itself? What kind of personal life would you have if you had a business like this one?

This kind of exercise is good to keep in mind when you're planning your business *and* your lifestyle. It helps you to see what you really want, what really matters to you, in your perfect business life because when planning your future, you not only need to know where you are now but also where you want to go.

This exercise can give you a lot of clues about what some of your values are, the obvious ones *and* the underlying ones. Was your office huge, with a couple of Monets on the walls? Was it slick and modern? Granny-chic? What did you wear to work in your dream day? Comfy jeans, a sweater, and clogs or an Armani suit and Christian Louboutins? Even though you weren't actively thinking about your bank balance in your dream business account, what you saw and how it made you feel can give you some clues as to what you really hope to accomplish.

WHAT MAKES YOU FEEL LIKE A REAL BUSINESS OWNER?

Some members of the Creative Collective weigh in on this eye-opening and mind-stretching topic.

"Ooh, financial stuff! That's when things stop being theoretical and start getting real. Now, I'm not a math/numbers person in any way/shape/form, but I really do enjoy the day I dedicate on the first weekday of every month to number crunching. That day, I block my calendar from any calls or sessions, and I go over the books from the previous month. It's actually fun to see the numbers grow, to see what's selling, and to go over what I'm investing in. Even if the numbers decline or something's not working as well as I expected it would (i.e., a product or service is underperforming), it's my time to put on my Nancy Drew hat and figure out how I can fix what's broken, and I look forward to that."
— **MICHELLE WARD**

"I love making deals and forming relationships with other organizations in my industry or in my community. Whether it's negotiating with a local hotel to get a block of complimentary rooms for a group of VIP guests at Fashion Week, finding sponsors for any of the conferences or events I help put together, speaking in front of large crowds, or making a pitch to another company that I'd like to design a product for, I absolutely relish all the opportunities I get as an entrepreneur to 'do business.' Taking command of a room is one of my strengths, and I love to challenge others in my industry and take risks. When I think of an archetypical 'business-person,' that is what I visualize, and I love having the opportunity to embody that person."
— **MEGAN HUNT**

"Shipping out my paintings. Packaging them up, writing the notes and blessings that go with each painting, and requesting the pickup on the UPS website. I agree with Seth Godin when he says, 'Artists ship.' That's when I feel most confident and in control of my work."
— JOLIE GUILLEBEAU

"Paying my two lovely assistants, treating them to lunch, and mentoring them in their own pursuits makes me feel like a regular ol' Daddy Warbucks. Ha! I also adore my customized postcards, business cards, and debit card, all of which are stylized like my website, with neon and jewel-tone polygons. Pretty foxy."
— ALEXANDRA FRANZEN

"I think my regular bookkeeping is the part that feels most businesslike to me. I have a really intimate relationship with my accounting system (I use QuickBooks). I keep my own books, but I have a wonderful and close relationship with my accountant who has taught me so much and who I go to when I'm confused or worried that I'm not putting something in the right category. Hiring an accountant was the best business decision I ever made."
— LISA CONGDON

"I think the decision making is what makes me feel most like a businessperson. Knowing that I will be the decider about everything concerning my business. I'm trying to keep a better focus on the decisions so that it still helps [my shop] Schmancy even if it's not a direct Schmancy activity / event / what have you. Basically, anything I do should also be to help Schmancy along, whether it's financially or more promotional."
— KRISTEN RASK

"Having my business license prominently displayed. That feels very official. Also, having a business credit card with my business name on it. That makes me feel pretty important at the post office and stuff."
— JESSIE OLESON

"Exhibiting at trade shows (like SURTEX) makes me feel the most like a businessperson because I get to interact with people in my industry, I have to actually get dressed and look nice (as opposed to wearing T-shirts and jeans working at home every day), and I get to wear a badge! I feel very official when I get to wear a badge!"
— JESSICA SWIFT

"Looking in the mirror to find my boss staring back at me. It's a pretty powerful and humbling feeling."
— SUE EGGEN

"It's never fun to enforce trademarks and copyrights, but I definitely feel like a businessperson when I have to do so. It's all part of looking out for your livelihood."
— NICOLE BALCH

"When I'm negotiating contracts or when I'm delegating roles to my employees or when I'm discussing the financial / tax accounting issues with my accountant!"
— KELLY RAE ROBERTS

FROM THE CREATIVE COLLECTIVE: JENA CORAY

If I knew then what I know now, I would have had more faith in myself and my decisions along the whole way of growing my business, and remembered to always, always trust my gut. The gut knows better than the head . . . every time.

PRACTICE MINDFULNESS AROUND FEELINGS

This brings us around to the topic of feelings. You might think that feelings shouldn't come into play when we're talking about business, but the truth is, your feelings are the most important business tool you've got.

Chances are you want to have your own business because you have a dream and your dream makes you feel a certain way. Maybe you crave the feeling of complete freedom or financial security, or you have a message or product that you feel will change the world. You can use your feelings as your guiding force, whether you're just beginning to plan what your business life is going to be about, in the middle of buying a business, or even closing one down. Pay attention to your feelings and what they are telling you. Your feelings will also come in handy when you're deciding if you should hire someone or if you should have a new website designed or whether you should expand your inventory. No matter what the business (or life!) decision is or needs to be, your feelings are really helpful.

One of the best things about having your very own business is that you have complete control. You're in charge of how hard you work, when and where you work, how much money you make or you're capable of making, and all of these pleasures are a direct result of your feelings.

FROM THE CREATIVE COLLECTIVE: JESSICA SWIFT

I work very intuitively and just move in the direction of whatever feels most exciting and fun.

So, yes, in business, as in all other aspects of your life, you need to pay attention to your feelings. Use them to guide you, to tell you when something is too good to be true, or if you're following your heart.

WHY ARE YOU IN BUSINESS? FORMULATE YOUR MISSION STATEMENT

Your dream is to accomplish something with your new or up-and-running venture — but what is that something, exactly? Determining your mission statement is one way to figure that out. Precisely how is having a mission statement useful? Well, for starters it is a clear definition of why you're in business. This will be of particular importance when you put together your business plan since a mission statement usually comes before anything else, other than the title page. When someone looks over your business plan, right from the start they'll have a good idea of what you're about. As they read

deeper into your plan, they'll know just exactly what it is you're trying to accomplish. They will more clearly understand your goals and your target market, or why you need some extra cash.

Being clear about exactly why you're in business can also be a big help to you personally. Being able to boil all that passion down into a couple of sentences will help keep you on track and provide you with a touchstone. If you don't know *why* you're in business to begin with, or what greater purpose your business serves, then you won't understand how to make other decisions.

BASIC MISSION STATEMENT QUESTIONS

To come up with your mission statement, you need to ask yourself some basic questions:

Why are you in business? Do you have a burning desire to bring beautiful graphic design to sad-looking websites across the Internet? Hey, nothing wrong with wanting to make the Internet a more beautiful place! Do you want to make new moms' lives easier by providing them with the perfect diaper bag that goes from car to stroller to shoulder with comfort and ease? Perfect! Moms across the world will thank you!

What is at the core of what you do, and why do you do it? To figure this out, take a look at your range of products and any and all income streams that you have. Do you knit dog sweaters and sell patterns? Do you do wedding photography and offer wedding websites, too? Or maybe you're a life coach who works with people one-on-one and offers e-courses on self-care.

When you take a look at the big picture of your business, what is the connection between everything you do and every product or service that you offer? What did you come up with? Is coaching or photography or knitting the common theme? You can begin to build your mission statement with that information.

EXERCISE

If you're hitting some mental snags trying to figure out this mission statement thing, get out your journal and make a flow chart. Make a list of all of your income streams, and then figure out what they have in common. Those details can help you whittle down what you do and what your overall mission is. If everything you make or teach or offer leads back to making the lives of stay-at-home parents or new business owners easier, then there you go.

Your mission statement is your chance to declare to the world just what is it you're all about, who you are, and where you're going. (Feel free to add some of your *future* goals into the mix while you're at it.) Your mission statement can be fluid. It's a good idea to look it over during your annual review to see if it's still in line with your company's values and if it still clearly defines the direction you're headed. You don't have to hide it away, though. Consider posting it on your website for your customers to see, or write it out on a big piece of poster board and hang it up above your workstation.

This is your MISSION! Your PURPOSE! This is why you're in business, baby! Say it loud, and say it proud!

By staying true to your mission statement and your goals/intentions, you'll be able to propel yourself forward with lightning speed.

FROM THE CREATIVE COLLECTIVE: MEGAN AUMAN

I'm a big advocate of having a tagline as a guiding principle for your business. (I prefer this because it's shorter and punchier than a mission statement.) My tagline for my design business is "Make a statement every day." This has really helped me understand what it is I do. Before, I thought I had to be limited to one material or one style, but now I know that if I focus on creating any kind of jewelry that's bold enough to make a statement but easy enough to wear every day, than it will be in line with my core mission.

CREATIVE THINKING
MISSION STATEMENTS

Here are some mission statements from Creative Collective people. You'll see how varied they are and maybe even get some inspiration!

"We believe a sense of humor, compassion, art, integrity, and pets are integral parts of a happy life. We believe in the importance of being inspired. We believe that the things that make you feel are just as important as the things that make you think. We believe in connecting with our neighbors next door and across the world. We strive to make art accessible to anyone and everyone because things of beauty enrich our lives in ineffable ways. We love what we do."
— **DEB THOMPSON**

"The mission of Princess Lasertron is to empower others to seek joy, create beauty every day, and be their best selves."
— **MEGAN HUNT**

"My mission is to empower passion-driven entrepreneurs to actualize their ideas, visions, and dreams while profiting abundantly from their work."
— **TARA GENTILE**

"The mission of CRAFTCAST is to produce cutting-edge online learning experiences in the creative realm, providing inspiration, knowledge, and access to a creative community."
— **ALISON LEE**

"Seeking Sweetness in Everyday Life. (The idea is that my business is a celebration of the little things that make life sweeter, both literally and figuratively. As a naturally inquisitive person, I consider myself the sweet sleuth who will hunt down these experiences, products, and create the artwork that will delight others.)"
— **JESSIE OLESON**

Chapter 4

TLC

The care and feeding of your business is a big deal. It's important to ensure that the things you need to do to survive and thrive live not just on your to-do list but also in your reality. For things to run as smoothly as possible and for you be to the happiest you can be, you need to keep an eye on all aspects of your business, and you are the most important component of your business. Your support system is comprised of many different factors; high on the list: how you take care of yourself and how you communicate with those closest to you, in both your personal and professional life.

No matter what you did for a living before you embarked on this wonderful adventure, you'll remember how a bad day at work affected you at home when your workday was done. The same is true when you work for yourself, only now those bad days can seem even more intense. When you're working for yourself, you will eat, breathe, and sleep your business, even when you're doing other things.

You're the boss now, and you can choose to have great working days every day. But it can take a little practice.

JUST SAY NO!

A wise woman I know once said something to the effect of, "Saying no makes more room for saying yes." In our daily lives, we are all responsible for a lot. Between family responsibilities, commitments to our friends and communities, things that the law and our governments want (or require) us to do, and tasks that we need to accomplish for our bodies and our health, well, it's possible

to run out of time to get everything done. Not to mention, in all of that daily-life stuff, you have to squeeze in that little thing known as your business! The answer to getting back some of your time and your sanity is to begin to say no.

You don't have to accept every challenge that comes along, you can skip a community obligation or two, and you don't have to do everything all by yourself.

Trust me, the sky won't fall if you personally don't have a finger in every pie. And it's definitely OK to turn down opportunities. Saying no is a tough skill to master. And, believe me, it takes practice. But the benefits you gain from protecting your time and energy are well worth the struggle.

Sure, it's very exciting to get asked to do more or contribute more, and you may feel pressure to say yes to everything that knocks on your door as a way of building your business. People may offer you "exposure" for your time or your product or you just may feel so gosh-darn happy that someone even considered you to work with them that you find yourself accepting everything that comes your way. Don't! Saying yes to everything can lead you off your track. Respectfully decline things that don't fit in with your vision or your goals. People say no to things all the time; it's how life works. Remember you're the boss now, and bosses don't always say yes to every request.

KEEP IT SIMPLE

Saying no or suggesting alternatives when asked to add one more thing to your plate is simple. Just smile and say that you can't do it. You don't even have to explain why! If your dance card is full to the max, just say so. You don't owe a big, grand explanation about how overworked/busy/stressed out you are to anyone.

Sometimes, when we offer up a big story of why something won't work for us, it can inadvertently cause other problems.

Usually we offer such a big and detailed account of why we're saying no because we have some guilt or other bad feelings lurking behind our decision. The thing is, if someone is asking you for something, it's most likely because they know you on some level. So if you present a bucket of problems as the thing that's standing in the way of you saying yes to their offer of extra work, theater tickets, chance to organize the town festival, or the fabbity-fab opportunity to catalog their inventory, they will most likely be compelled to try to help you solve the issue standing in the way of you saying yes. So if you want to avoid their efforts at problem solving, just be gracious and simply say no.

People will still ask you for help or to be a part of things in the future. Turning down one collaboration doesn't mean you'll never get another offer to work with someone else, and not going to lunch with your studio mate when you've got a looming deadline doesn't mean you'll never get asked to have a burrito in the park again.

DECLINE GRACEFULLY

To get you started on getting comfortable with saying no, here are a few examples:

➤ Thanks for asking, but I can't commit to anything extra right now. Check back with me in six months if you're still looking for some help. Your idea sounds great, and I wish you a lot of luck.

➤ I'm very pleased that you thought of me for this project, but I'm not taking on anything new right now. Actually, Person-We-Both-Know may be interested in something like this.

➤ You know how much I love burritos in the park! But today's just not good for me. Could you bring one back for me, though? I'm so swamped today, I can't leave at all.

➤ Thank you, but no.

EXERCISE 1

Think of something you were asked to do recently that you said yes to but wish you had said no to. OK? Now replay the situation in your head, and this time say no. How does it play out? Do you feel better saying no? What was the person's reaction in your mind movie? If it was negative, could you have phrased your refusal in a better way? Offered less of an explanation as to why you were saying no, which maybe would have give them less of a reason to solve your issue?

EXERCISE 2

Loosely keep track of the things you do on a daily or weekly basis. How many of them are you doing for other people? How many of them do you wish you didn't have to do? Are any of them time sucks that cause you stress? Is there any way you can avoid doing them next week?

WHO CARES? YOU DO!

Self-care. Just what does that mean exactly? Self-care is an old concept, getting a wonderful makeover by community leaders these days. I can't seem to read a business blog or follow another coach on Twitter without getting a daily dose of self-care tips, and I'm so grateful! Self-care is very important to your success as a businessperson and to you just as, um, a person. It's true that if you don't take care of yourself, nothing else will be taken care of.

I'm sure you've heard that old cliché about the airplane and the oxygen mask, right? You know, you're on the plane and you're told that you must first put on *your* oxygen mask and then your child's mask. And the reason is obvious: if you take care of yourself first, you could then take care of the child. But if you take care of the child first, they may be unable to take care of you if something goes wrong. This is how your business works, too.

If you're not able to take care of your most basic needs, like eating well, sleeping well, and managing other life responsibilities that you can't get out of no matter what, you won't be able to manage your business well. Taking care of yourself means you can take care of your responsibilities, hopes, and dreams.

FROM THE CREATIVE COLLECTIVE: MICHELLE WARD

Be you. Sure, it so sounds like it's cheating, but honestly, it's what brought me here. I embraced my uniquity early on (thankfully, my background as a musical-theater performer taught me the importance of that, and I brought that lesson into my business), and I think that, if I hadn't, I would have blended into the kamillion other life coaches out there. I'm not saying to make yourself weird for weirdness' sake, but I am saying that you need to broadcast whatever it is that makes you uniquely you, and don't be afraid to isolate anyone in the process. I promise that, if you express your uniquity — wherever you are, whatever you say, whatever you write — you'll attract the right people to you and be able to build your business on the people you work best with or who love your products the most.

Now, of course, everyone's life is different. I can't know exactly what your daily life is like or know all the details of your business. No one can really be in your shoes other than you. And no one can take care of you like you can.

SELF-CARE BASICS

To make things easier on your sweet self, keep the following in mind:

Get enough sleep. Sleep needs vary for each individual. My husband, Eric, needs his full 8 hours. My mother, Janis, functions on fewer than 5 hours a night most days. I'm in the middle, happy and functional at around 6 hours, better with 7 or 8 hours, but I *can* work on 4. Figure out what your personal minimum amount of sleep is, and then make sure you get it.

Keep hydrated. This is a no-brainer, and I'm sure you know that keeping your water intake up is very, very important. So I won't go on about it. Just go get yourself a glass of water and drink it up while you read the next few pages of this book. Then get yourself another glass.

Know your limits. Knowing what causes you a great deal of stress with your business or knowing what makes you avoid tasks or jobs that need to get done is another great way to put self-care into practice. Once you know what stresses you out, figure out why, and then think about ways to make it easier on yourself. If you dislike writing sales copy or doing promotion, or whatever your personal bane may be, think of some ways to make it easier on yourself, and then put them into practice. Maybe meet a friend at a coffee shop, and you can each work on your dreaded tasks at the same time while enjoying each other's company and a good cup of java.

Make time for yourself. Sounds simple, yet it's often harder to accomplish than you might think. Consider taking some time each week and making it really special. For example, if you love searching online marketing places for inspiration or you can spend hours on Pinterest (ahem, this one works for me!), then set aside time each working day at a time when you most need it to allow yourself this treat.

For example, I begin to fall apart every day around 3:00 p.m. This is a productivity trigger time for me. No matter how much of a roll I'm on, it seems that around 3:00 p.m., I start to slow down, even when I don't want to. Do you have a time of day like this? I've learned to recognize my own signs of slacking off and what to do when it happens. When I start noticing that things are taking me even longer than usual or that I've checked my email approximately 20 times in the past twenty minutes, I know it must be 3:00 p.m. or close to it. This is when I allow myself an uninterrupted break. I set my timer for twenty minutes, and I jump on my trampoline or browse my favorite websites or just doze off for a quick nap. This break really helps to reinvigorate me. Twenty minutes works for me because it's not a long enough time for me to get out of work mode, and I can't really do anything big and distracting, but it's very nice to take a break without any guilt.

Be clear with those boundaries! To stay in touch with your business and

FROM THE CREATIVE COLLECTIVE: DEB THOMPSON

When I feel stressed, my focus tends to get very small, and my thinking gets rigid. Early on, I assumed that since I was pursuing a lifelong dream, I wouldn't experience stress in the same way as I did in my former job. Not so! My advice: Learn stress-reduction techniques. For me, exercise and meditation work well, but I know there are lots of options, and it's helpful to know early on what works. Since I often walk to work, I try to use that time to picture myself and my business more expansively. When that doesn't work, I take my mother's advice, which is to just keep moving forward.

your feelings, perhaps consider making one day a week off-limits to tasks that take up a lot of your time or creative energy. Say, you decide not to take phone calls or return business-related emails on Thursdays. Just simply let your customers or clients know that Thursday is your planning day or your catch-up day (the day of the week that you attend to the smaller details of your business) and you'll get back to them on Friday or whatever your next working day is. This kind of freedom to focus on what you haven't been able to accomplish, without your phone ringing or the pressure to return correspondence, can be very freeing and an easy way to make sure you feel taken care of and in touch with why you're doing all of this to begin with. Try it!

FAMILY MATTERS

And speaking of taking care of yourself, one of the very best ways you can ensure your success and those feel-good vibes is to make sure that you have an excellent support system in place. I'm talking about your family. The people who depend on you each day to function as a family member may not understand as easily when you need to function as a businessperson, especially if you work from home. If your family is used to you being readily available to them, or, say, your dining room actually functions as a dining room for family-night dinner and board games, and all of the sudden it looks like a shipping and receiving center or your own personal post office,

FROM THE CREATIVE COLLECTIVE: **KELLY RAE ROBERTS**

Surround yourself with people who support you; people who understand the long work hours, the importance of making dreams happen, and people who share their resources and community with you.

confusion may ensue. This could lead to you not getting the support that you truly need to make your business thrive.

Don't sweat it too much because there is hope. Talking with your family about what their needs are and what their expectations are of you is key. Perhaps your chore schedule will have to be switched up, or maybe the people you live with will need to take some of your household burdens away from you so you can grow your business. You'll need to be really clear and upfront about what your needs are and what you expect from your family before you take a big leap into changing or expanding your business.

ALL ABOARD

If the people who matter to you the most are on board with the direction you're going in, they will be invested in your success. And when the people around you are invested in your success, you'll be more successful, so really it's a win-win situation.

Most of us at some point in life have had to make sacrifices for others. Maybe you had a baby and found yourself trying to squeeze all your work in during baby's naps. Or perhaps your life partner was going after their PhD, and you had to take on the household chores while they toiled away at the library all day and all night. In a perfect world, you wouldn't have minded one bit rearranging

COLLABORATION

If you're using family savings or cashing in your 401(k) to fund your business, you must make absolutely sure that anyone in your life who depends on you and your earnings is on board with the decisions you're making. Your business plan will help in these situations. If you're able to clearly express what you're doing and why, chances are those around you from whom you from really want approval will more easily be able to be on the same page as you.

your life or schedule to support or tend to those you love, but, truthfully, we don't live in perfect worlds.

Unwelcome resentment can crop up at any old time; it just happens. For obvious reasons, you'll want to avoid this if at all possible.

One way to keep your family on your side is to constantly be in communication with them about how your business is doing and what you're working on. Filling them in on all the details, the ins and outs, the highs and lows, will ensure that they really understand what's going on. More importantly, they'll understand exactly just what it is that you're working so hard to accomplish and why your attention sometimes seems to be divided.

No one likes to feel unsupported, and if you begin to feel this way, take steps to fix it as soon as you can.

EXERCISE
When you do your numbers or update your press file or track your new customers or clients at the end of the month, make a small official report to share with your family. Include them in on your progress.

Treat them like business partners in small ways or like silent investors, which in fact they sort of are. Let them know where your business stands.

TAKE YOURSELF ON A CREATIVE RETREAT

A creative retreat is an excellent way to recharge your batteries, and we can all use a nice recharge from time to time. It's best to have some objectives in mind before you retreat. If you want to think of new products, write a new kind of song, or expand your design ideas, getting yourself outside of your normal routine is a great way to make room for new ideas and concepts. You never know what will inspire a new idea so be as open-minded as possible when it comes to new possibilities.

Going on a retreat does not mean that you have to book yourself into a spa for the weekend (although if that's what sounds good to you, by all means book away, my friend). You can retreat in many, many different kinds of ways. I once asked an artist friend if I could work in her painting studio for two days. Just being in someone else's creative space while I wrote was an amazing creative experience for me. Being surrounded by all of her supplies and canvases and even the way it all smelled was enough of a change from my own studio that the ideas came flooding in.

Do you have a favorite place where you like to hang out? Try spending some time there each week with the goal in mind to freshen up your outlook. If you normally hang out at a favorite park or coffee shop just to write blog entries, switch it up. Next time you head there, take your journal and a favorite inspirational book. Relax and read and be ready to jot down anything promising that pops into your head.

But sometimes when I need a mental break, I drive. Getting into my car with Martha Beck on my iPod and taking a scenic route often sparks something in me that I wasn't able to access when I was sitting at my desk with my laptop open in front of me.

EXERCISE

Set aside some time to just think about your business. I know, you think about your business all the time, duh, but I mean just free-form think about things. Pick a goal and just brainstorm it in as many ways as you can. Allow yourself to think big, wild thoughts. Don't put any expectations or pressure on yourself during your retreat time. Whether you take an hour to do this or a long weekend, the point is to empty your brain of worries and outcomes, and let new things brew. Think of it as a "re-treat," a treat for your business.

Chapter 5

GOALS AND INTENTIONS

Setting goals is the perfect time to do my all-time favorite thing: DREAM. I believe there is no better way to get in touch with yourself and what you want for your personal life and your creative business than by dreaming. Dreams will lead you to your big ideas, which will lead you to your intentions, which will help you set goals.

Dreaming is the perfect way to figure out what you want and where you want to go and who you want to be. And dreaming BIG is wonderful. It makes you feel good and helps you discover things you didn't know about yourself. I hope you're able to spend some time each day dreaming a bit. I sure do. It keeps me going! Here's where that creative visualization exercise we did in chapter 3 will come in handy.

KEEP YOURSELF HONEST

There is a difference between dreaming big and inflating your abilities. Dreaming big is *mucho* important. But being honest about your abilities, and having a realistic time frame in which to accomplish your dreams, are just as important. By overestimating what you're able to accomplish and how long you think it would take you to accomplish it, you're setting yourself up for failure. And that's no good.

Building a business can take a long time, which is totally A-OK. Don't put a crazy amount of pressure on yourself to get things done (or get things done by X date) or to see your bank balance grow. Take your time and make sure that what you're working on is making you happy.

CHECKING IN

Keep yourself under control by reviewing your intentions and checking in with yourself from time to time. Does what you're doing feel right? Is a project or collaboration truly in line with where you want to go and who you want to become? If not, it's OK to wipe the slate clean and start again. If something doesn't feel right, do a gut check, and then trust your gut.

Sometimes projects, ideas, and products just don't turn out the way we envisioned them. That's normal, and it happens in all areas in every part of our lives, not just business. Have you ever made a big dinner from scratch, and after all the effort, it just didn't taste good? That doesn't mean that you failed or, worse, will go hungry for the rest of your life just because one meal wasn't as delicious as you had hoped. It just means you do something different next time, like add in your own special ingredient or plan a completely different meal. The same rules apply to your business.

DETERMINE GOALS

Deciding on your business goals is one of the biggest responsibilities, not to mention one of the most *fun* responsibilities, you have. Goals are really amazing things. They give you focus and set your course. I'd like you to think back to when you very first started your creative-business journey, regardless of whether it was 10 minutes ago or 10 years ago. You had goals, right? Possibly one of those goals was to learn more about

business planning, and so you happened on this book.

At one point, did you want to open an Etsy store, and now you have one? Did you want to learn a new skill that would advance your abilities, and now you're the master of that skill? If so, good for you! You need to recognize that you reach goals all the time. And, yes, the small ones count. Even if you set a goal at some point to, say, wake up a half hour earlier than your family so you can get some work done *and you actually do it*, you have accomplished a goal. See how good you are it? You are a goal-accomplishing machine!

Pretty much, you can't get anything done if you don't have goals.

FROM THE CREATIVE COLLECTIVE: **ALISON LEE**

Decision making is second nature to entrepreneurs. Knowing the power of making a decision is your strongest asset. Once its power is experienced firsthand, it is very addicting. Goals and objectives are made by lots of smaller decisions. Writing down goals and objectives makes them even more powerful.

Why? Simple. If you don't have goals, you don't have anything to work toward.

EXERCISE
I'd like you to pick up your journal, and take a walk down memory lane. Make a list of all the goals you've had since you decided to be a creative business owner. Now circle all the goals that you've already accomplished.

GOALS VERSUS INTENTIONS

You may be wondering what the difference is between a goal and an intention. To put it in its simplest terms, let's just say that an intention is the grandest statement that you can make, and the goals line up to support the intention. An intention is the end result of your goal, if you will. An intention is a statement of fact, what you *intend* to do. A series of goals will help you make your intention come true. Got that? Here are some examples of intentions:

➤➤ In the next four years, I will grow my business to the point where I can work for myself full-time, running my successful creative business.

➤➤ I will master my accounting software (that cost me an arm and a leg!) in the next six months.

➤➤ I will find a space to run my business from that works for me and my business needs.

➤➤ I will find support for the parts of my business that are overwhelming me so that I can focus on what I do best.

The intention is the desired end result. The intention is like a FACT. Intentions help you keep your overall focus. Intentions don't have to be big and scary, though. If you have no idea where you want to go, just start with some smaller intentions and see how it goes. Like:

➤➤ I will get up an hour earlier each day to practice yoga before I get ready for work.

➤➤ I will increase my followers on Twitter by 20 percent over the next four months.

➤➤ I will challenge my creative skills by trying something new just for the fun of it.

Just by putting it out there, stating the fact of what you truly want to accomplish, can help set your creative-business dreams in motion. You may notice your brain nudging you to lay out your yoga mat by your favorite window before you go to bed so that it's waiting for you in the morning. You may all of the sudden have the desire to finally tweet to someone you've been following for a long time but have perhaps been too shy about reaching out to before. You might find yourself opening up that new software instead of your RSS feed.

INTENTIONS + GOALS = SUCCESS

Now let's add some goals to enable all of these wonderful intentions. Let's try this one that I previously mentioned:

INTENTION

I will find support for the parts of my business that are overwhelming me so that I can focus on what I do best.

GOALS

➤ Make a list of all the things I do on a daily basis to make my business run. To achieve this, I'll keep a detailed work log for two weeks.

SETTING INTENTIONS

Setting intentions is a great way to begin planning for your business. One of my favorite philosophies (I didn't invent this concept, but instead learned it from one of my virtual mentors) is to begin where you want to end up and then work backward. I can honestly tell you that this little trick is one of the best ones that I have in my handmade bag of business-coaching tricks. When we know where we want to end up, we won't be surprised when things, good or bad, come our way, and we'll have a better sense of when we're wasting our time and efforts on projects that we don't really want to work on.

- Find out how long a project really takes and exactly how many steps it takes to complete something. To achieve this, I'll keep a detailed work log of one project from beginning to end.

- Investigate the possibility of hiring an intern. To achieve this, ask friends and associates who work with interns about their experiences.

- Consider the idea of working with a virtual assistant (VA). Make a list of duties I would give to a VA, and investigate what VAs generally charge.

- Write up a mock job description. Ascertain what I would have employees do for me.

- Determine which things are necessary for my business and also those that I don't enjoy doing or am not really good at.

These goals support the intention. By actively working on these goals, the end result will be accomplished. See how that works?

You can use your intentions to make sure you keep your business on track. As you move forward through your business plan and in your daily business life, your intentions will help you to focus on what you really want to be doing.

KEEPING ON COURSE

It's easy to get sidetracked. Lots of opportunities will be heading your way. Everything from collaborations with creative cohorts, to new accounts, to things you haven't even dreamed of yet are in your future. Keeping in touch with your intentions is a way to stay true to yourself.

Distractions are always going to be plentiful. Having a strong foundation for your business, and a clear end result in mind, will help you stay on course. When something does arise, such as a teaching prospect or a chance to guest blog on a popular website, or even a press opportunity that seems too good to be true, a quick check of where you want to go by reviewing your intentions and goals may be just what you need.

When an opportunity presents itself that you're interested in checking out, take a look at what you're considering. Does it feel right to you? Where does it fit into your plan? Is it going to move you forward or distract you, pushing something back as you shift things to make room for this new project?

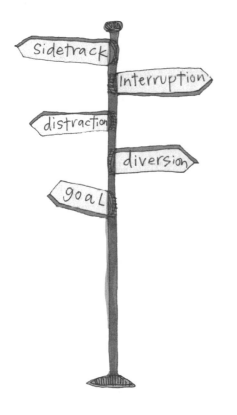

MAKE REASONABLE GOALS

At this point, you should have a better understanding about intentions and goals and how they work together. But come on. You've been setting goals and either reaching them or letting go of them forever, right?

Right.

If you are really good about achieving all of your goals, super! I'd love to know your secret. Honestly, in the past I always had trouble meeting my goals, and I know now it's because they were often too big. As far as I was concerned, I just had a goal, and that was that. Like writing a book. About a million years ago, when I was a teenager, I said to myself, "When I grow up, I'm going to write books." And that was that.

Every year that I didn't write a book, I would feel bad about it. I was constantly moaning and groaning to anyone who would listen about how I knew I was simply meant to be an author, and why wasn't I writing a book yet?

CREATIVE THINKING
ON SETTING GOALS

"My goals are really centered around what I enjoy doing and what sounds really exciting to me. I don't want to spend any more time than absolutely necessary doing things to make money that I don't enjoy."
— LISA CONGDON

"I think having a big end goal to visualize helps you move down your path in a focused way. Use that vision as a gauge for what you do in your business. Allow that vision to change and morph and grow as your business grows. Don't look at it as a static image that will never change; use it as something that you get to interact with, to inspire you, and keep you excited about where your business is going!"
— JESSICA SWIFT

"I have a poster in my studio of our goals for each quarter. Looking at it every day keeps me focused on what I can do to get us there."
— MEGAN HUNT

"I come up with goals by just concentrating on what I really want. Often, we don't give our personal desires enough weight because we're afraid of being selfish. If you have confidence in your motives and the greater value of your work, it's easier to also act out of personal desire. Generating goals based on personal desire but grounded in community value will help you find the motivation you need to execute them."
— TARA GENTILE

"I like to sit down and review my yearly goals now and then. Where am I? What do I need to work on? What have I accomplished so far? I'm often surprised by what I've actually done but have forgotten about."
— JOLIE GUILLEBEAU

Well, my friend, it's because that is *all* I had: the goal to write a book. I never really had any ideas about what said book would be about or even how one got the "job" of author. For a long time I suspected that you either needed to know how to cast spells on publishing types, or there was a book fairy that only insiders knew about who floated into people's bedrooms at night and sprinkled them with author dust, and then, *WHAM–O!*, they wrote a book.

If only I had known way back when that my declaration of "I'm going to write a book" was really my intention, I could have set myself up with a bunch of reasonable goals to help me get there a whole lot sooner. Once I *did* figure that out though… Whoa Nelly! There was no stopping me. And now here I am!

WHAT *IS* A REASONABLE GOAL?

So what exactly *is* a reasonable goal? To me, a reasonable goal is one that you can actually attain. Have you ever made a to-do list and included a few things you had already done or knew for sure you would get to,

just so you could cross something off right away? I am famous for starting each day's to-do with "wake up" and "make coffee" and "walk dogs," which, really, are all things that *will* happen in my day even if nothing else does. But I love being able to check each of those boxes and then cross them out. (I know: weird, right? I am a box checker and a crosser off-er!)

All I'm suggesting is that instead of setting a definitive-but-hard-to-accomplish goal, try setting ones that you know are doable. That doesn't mean that you shouldn't dream big or challenge yourself. Not at all!

The more you break that intention down, the more likely you'll end up with many, many goals or things you can accomplish that help you get to that final goal … which is your big intention. See?

Your goals should be your friends; they should excite you, and you should look forward to working toward them. Goals are not chores.

In fact, if any begin to feel like a chore, you need to reevaluate. If a goal seems too hard, make it easier.

I like to set a goal and then break it down into smaller tasks, and then break those tasks down even further until I have something I can do *in this moment*. To analyze the elements from top to bottom:

Intention. (Big, grand, ultimate objective! Woo-hoo!)

Goal. (Steps you'll take to get to the intention.)

Task. (Teeny-tiny proactive things you do to reach the goal.)

STRATEGY IN ACTION

Here's an example of just how that strategy works:

INTENTION

Relocate my business outside of my home.

GOAL

Find a space that is affordable and will make running my business easier. (This goal supports my intention.)

TASKS

➤➤ Talk to other creative people I know, and ask where they work.

➤➤ Write down the phone number posted on that beautiful building downtown with the sign that says **Artists Spaces for Rent.**

"Don't let best get in the way of better." I've tried to track down the source of that quote, unsuccessfully, but it's advice that I need to remind myself of often. I'm a perfectionist, and I find myself putting off tasks until I can complete them perfectly. But what ends up happening then is that they don't get done at all. Done is better than perfect.

- Call the number, and ask if they still have any available spaces.
- Check Craigslist every other day for studios.
- Review my budget and determine how much I could comfortably pay in rent.
- Make a detailed list of how my business will change if I am working out of the house.

All of these tasks will help me reach my goal, which will in turn allow me to realize my intention. Neat, huh? And because some of these tasks are so small, I can begin working on them as soon as today. I could pull up Craigslist or drive by that loft building on my way to my afternoon meeting.

The point of this is not only do I have a bunch of things to work on that support my big dream, but also the process has untangled the big messy heap of jumbled thoughts that live in my head surrounding working out of my house.

All of those little tasks are reasonable and easy enough to do, yet if I don't accomplish one of them, the whole thing won't fall apart. And if I do accomplish them all, eventually

I'll realize my intention. Curiously, while I am accomplishing these goals and tasks, I may discover that the intention I'm working toward isn't what I really want after all. Believe me, that has happened to me more than once.

KEEP TRACK OF YOUR GOALS AND INTENTIONS

How you choose to track your goals and intentions is up to you. I happen to be a list maker by nature. I solve most of my problems and dream most of my dreams by making lists. But that's just me. You may have an entirely different method.

No matter what works for you, I highly recommend that you keep a copy of your goals and intentions somewhere. A dedicated notebook or journal may work for you. A white board in your office or workspace might be what you need. In any regard, writing them down will help you put them into action. Once you have taken the time and carved out the space to actually write these suckers down or type them up, they will be around, out there, and there is power in that. Truly there is.

When you're actually ready to put your business plan together, keep a list of your intentions in the plan. Keep another copy somewhere accessible that has your breakdown of goals, and your tasks can make their way onto your to-do list. You don't have to go around sharing them with people or plastering them on your refrigerator where your room-mate can gaze at them while drinking your orange juice straight out of the carton in the middle of the night. But just by virtue of having them close to you, somewhere easy to access, it will help you keep your focus. And that is just good business.

KNOW WHAT AND WHERE YOUR GOALS ARE

Your creative business is important. You are important. Your intentions and goals are important.

These goals are like tiny seeds that will grow into your future success, and you need to make sure you not only know *what* your goals are but also *where* they are.

I personally use a sketchbook. That way I can glue or tape related items beside the goals, like a business card or a picture that gave me an idea for my business. This not only makes reviewing my goals fun, but it's also a great way for me to keep in touch with them and thereby keep in touch with myself (and I am often

FROM THE CREATIVE COLLECTIVE: JOLIE GUILLEBEAU

Take small steps consistently. Do something every single day to make a little progress toward your goal.

hard to get in touch with). I generally use two pages for each intention and the goals and tasks that go along with it. It's helpful to me to be able to make notes and add things as I go along. Two pages give me lots of room to spread my dreams out, and most of the time I wind up needing additional space, so I just freshen everything up when I make a new layout.

Intentions and the goals that support them can be scary — and that's a good thing. A big goal can stretch your comfort zone, which can lead to amazing things. Keep setting intentions, and keep stretching yourself. Your business is only going to get bigger and better, thanks to your hard work.

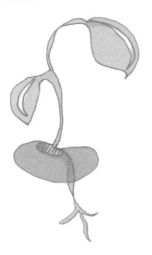

WHEN A DREAM BECOMES ... LESS OF A DREAM

Here's an example of some goal-setting and intention work I did with a client:

When I first went into business as a creative-business coach, one of my first clients was a gentleman I'll call Adam. This wonderful, talented fellow had a ceramics business that was beginning to grow at a really rapid rate, growth that was unexpected and quite sudden. Some of his pieces had been for sale in a local boutique home-goods store, and then he participated in a group art show in his town. It so happened that a reporter came by the show, saw Adam's work, and ended up writing about him. Before he knew it, he was up to his eyeballs in orders, which at first made him really happy. As time went on, though, he felt considerably less happy, putting in extensive hours to fill all those new orders while still working at his full-time day job. Adam was beginning to feel a bit jaded about his business. He lost sight of what he really wanted and instead felt bogged down by his success.

Adam suddenly questioned whether he really and truly wanted a full-time crafts business. Here he had spent so much time dreaming about building a business that would allow him to work for himself and work on his art, but when he got a taste of what it would be like, he began thinking that maybe it wouldn't be like what he had dreamed it would be after all.

What the heck does this have to do with goals and intentions? you may be asking. Hang on, and I think you'll see where I'm going with this.

Adam had thought he wanted to be a full-time ceramist. He had thought he wanted to run a business of his own. He had thought he would be happy filling orders all day and night. But he wasn't. Surprise!

It didn't take me long to realize that Adam was simply overwhelmed. As I said, he had a full-time job, which he needed because he also had a family of four to support, and his day job provided their health care and a steady, reliable paycheck. Before his newfound success, his free time was spent at his kiln and his wheel because he loved making pottery. But his love was fading fast as he struggled to keep up with the new demands that came along with that very same success.

What we needed to do was figure out what he really wanted and then how he was going to get it. Ah! Easy-peasy . . . right?

First, Adam and I worked on his goals and intentions. Exactly what did he see for himself down the road? What did he really, really, *really* want from his business? Once he figured that out, things began to immediately improve.

Adam needed to set his intentions. Once he did so, his goals fell into place, and his tasks became manageable. He decided that he wanted to pursue his ceramics business full-time, and to do that, he had to figure out how to make it work. But the point is, once he had the intention to quit his day job and become a full-time potter, things got better for him immediately.

Deb owns an art gallery that also sells very thoughtful product lines for the home. I have been a customer of hers for many years, and the way she has her business, Nahcotta, set up is my favorite brick-and-mortar business model. She gets to work one-on-one with wonderful artists from around the world, and she sells other beautiful things. Her art shows are online for everyone to see.

Pretty much, I think she has a perfect business space and a wonderful career. But she didn't just wake up one day the owner of a popular gallery; she started somewhere completely different and worked toward where she wanted to be.

What is the best part of owning a successful gallery?
I've developed wonderful friendships with some of the artists that I work with and watched with great respect and admiration as their careers have taken off. If we play even a small role in supporting an artist so that he or she may continue to do work that makes them deeply happy, I find that thrilling.

How do you balance your personal life and your business life?
Juggling my work and personal life has been enormously challenging for me. I have swung fairly far in both directions and have had to become much more intentional about creating a healthy balance. Often, I will try to totally disconnect during my time off by leaving my phone or laptop at home for short periods. Owning a business can mean that you live and breathe it night and day. Nahcotta is certainly an integral part of who I am, but I'm learning that it's not *all* of who I am.

Have you made any big mistakes in running your business? If so, what did you take away from the experience that helped your business become stronger?

I've made *hundreds* of mistakes, some big, some small, but I think they all played a role in getting [me] where I am today. I didn't trust my instincts enough in the beginning, and I wasn't smart about how and where I spent money. I used all of my savings to open and run Nahcotta in the early years instead of putting some of it away and getting a line of credit. Not having that safety net is what caused me to use credit cards early on. But that experience taught me more about how I approach money and how to run a lean business than I could have imagined.

Chapter 6

BENCHMARKS

Setting benchmarks is a good way to define what success looks like to you, and is an important step in the business-planning process. Success doesn't always mean that you have accomplished everything you set out to do. It can look and feel like anything you want. Sometimes, if I just get two paragraphs written, I feel successful. Success can be fluid and changeable if that works for you. For me, if I feel good about what I've done during the day, with how I've spent my time, I feel successful. And that can go a long way.

MEASURING YOUR SUCCESS

How do you measure your success? Since it has a lot to do with your intentions and goals, only you can decide what success looks like to you and your business. I'd like you to take your journal and look at one of your favorite intentions. (Perhaps it's something like quitting your day job and working for yourself within the next year.) Now work on the goals underneath that intention, and then break a few of your goals down into tasks. If you complete a few of the tasks, you have come that much closer to reaching the goal, and you're that much closer to realizing the intention, which means you're being successful.

Another way to measure your success is to determine how you want to feel. Take some time and make a list of the feelings you want to experience from your business. Your list may look something like this:

Free   Self-reliant
Happy   Secure
Abundant   Creative
Exuberant   Accomplished

Check in with yourself from time to time. Is your business making you feel how you want to feel, which is to

FROM THE CREATIVE COLLECTIVE: TARA GENTILE

I focus on results. I think about the money, credibility, relief, excitement, or pride that I'm going to achieve or feel when I'm back on track. It's not enough to think about the end goal; I need to be able to touch and taste every bit of the result. Once I do that, accomplishing things becomes easy.

say, fulfilled? If so, you're achieving your personal definition of success. Congratulations! If not, figure out why. What could you do to improve the state of your feelings?

THINK AHEAD

While you're busy making that list of feelings, spend some time thinking about where you'd like your business to be in six months from now, one year from now, and then five years from now. I know. These are age-old questions, asked in many job interviews and by parents the world over, but there is a good purpose behind them. Thinking ahead will keep your planning muscles in shape. Once you take a good look at your long-term plans, you'll see some intentions and goals take shape. Reviewing these monthly or quarterly or even yearly will help you know if you're on track.

It's important to measure your success because it's necessary to know what's working and what isn't. If you have been pursuing a line, a project, or a service but you're just not getting the results you want, it's definitely time to reevaluate.

FROM THE CREATIVE COLLECTIVE: MICHELLE WARD

I have a yearly financial goal that I work into my spreadsheets on a monthly and annual basis (related to how far away I am to that target), and I came to that number by figuring what's realistic to hit and raising it about 20 percent. That way I have something to reach for while still believing it's not gonna take a parallel universe or a lottery win to get me to that number.

Measuring Your Success 87

WHAT DOES SUCCESS LOOK LIKE?

Say one of your ultimate intentions is to become a gazillionaire. You want to be filthy, stinking rich. So you have an intention that looks like this:

I want to be a GAZILLIONAIRE!

Just because that gazillion dollars isn't in your pocket right now, or likely won't be even a year from now, doesn't mean you aren't successful. But ponder this: The more reasonable and easily attainable the financial goals you set for yourself are, the more successful you'll be. For example, if your intention is to increase your profit by 15 percent over the next three months rather than, say, doubling it, chances are you'll feel better about the direction your business is heading, and the boost you get when your intention is manifested will be huge.

FROM THE CREATIVE COLLECTIVE: TARA GENTILE

My plans for my business are almost completely driven by objectives. I believe in setting really spacious goals that allow for victory in "failure" and flexibility in "destination." I create objectives around income, influence, experience, and personal freedom. I come up with goals by just concentrating on what I really want. Generating goals based on personal desire but grounded in community value will help you find the motivation you need to execute them.

EXERCISE

Think about what success means to you. Really, really think about it. In your journal, write up a personal definition that you can return to again and again if you need or want to.

Likewise, think about what failure looks like to you. What would have to happen for you to feel like your business was failing? Write that down, too. If you ever feel like things are way off track, look back on your personal definition of failure. Compare it to what you're going through. Chances are, according to your very own definition, your business is not failing.

CALCULATING SUCCESS ONE STEP AT A TIME

Consider some areas of your business that can offer easily calculable success. As always, when trying out something new, you can make things easier on yourself by starting small. Setting small benchmarks, little check-in points, can assist you when you're deciding if you're on track or not.

Remember how I mentioned starting at the end, figuring where you want to be, and then working your way backward to the beginning? Let's put that exercise into practice by imagining where you want to end up and then work backward to get there. We'll use social media as an example. Let's say you want to improve your social media connections, which ties into your marketing and sales. Specifically, you want to increase your followers on Twitter by a thousand people. So imagine that you're already there, and then work backward toward where you actually are right now. By retracing your steps, so to speak, you'll discover what you need to do to get to where you want to go.

SPECIFIC STEPS

Here are some specific steps you can take, using social media as an example:

INTENTION

By the end of the year, I will increase my Twitter audience by 1,000 people.

I'm usually focused on growth. How can I reach X number of subscribers to my blog, how can I hit X number of sales, and so on. I look at what's possible, based on past statistics, then try to push myself to go a bit further.

GOALS

- Connect further with like-minded businesspeople by responding to their tweets more.

- Post useful and relevant content.

- Post links to my best blog posts.

- Add a tweet button to my website so that others can tweet links from my site with ease.

TASKS

- Ask a pal how they installed the tweet button on their website.

- Follow the links others tweet, and retweet the best ones, as time permits.

- When I'm reading new blogs, look for people's Twitter links.

- Connect more with people who follow me.

- Respond to strangers when they communicate with me.

HOW SUCCESS WILL BE MEASURED

Record my current number of followers, and increase the number by 25 percent every three months. I'll notate my calendar as a reminder.

See? You set an intention and some goals, and then listed some doable tasks. Since you notated your calendar to check in with your intention in three months' time, you can decide then if your tasks are really helping you reach your goals. After three months, you could decide that your intention was too ambitious for the amount of time you spend reaching out through social media. Or you may have already added those thousand Twitter followers. If so, you know that your intention has been met and so you are ready to set a new one.

I set fresh intentions, raise my financial threshold, and revisit my service structures whenever I've hit a leaden blockade, either energetically or revenue-wise. During my first year as a full-time entrepreneur, I had to stop and recalibrate several times. Trial and error is a fussy, messy business. But that's the nature of creating something out of nothing. Intelligent experimentation. These days things are ticking along much more elegantly. I'm no longer in perpetual "launch mode." I feel grounded and graceful in my business. I suspect I'll spruce up my master plan in six months or so. Or whenever I get hit with a bolt of brilliance that changes everything, all over again.

PERIODIC CHECKUPS

Periodically checking in on your progress is essential to your success. At regular intervals, look over your business plan, see what areas you'd like to monitor closely, and decide how you'd like to assess your progress.

Oftentimes people make things hard on themselves by reviewing things just once or twice a year or when things are going poorly. But if you set aside time to review your business plan every couple of months, you may well avoid some heartache and some pitfalls because you'll be able to notice details and kinks before they become problems. Conversely, you'll pick up on things that are working well that you may not have noticed, and maybe your next big idea will come from tracking your stats.

Chapter 7

GET SOME HELP!

Hopefully right about now you're getting a clear(er) perspective on just what it is you want to create and how you want to work. And as you go through the process of starting or expanding your business and creating your business plan, there may be times when you need some help to reach those clarified expectations.

SAY IT LOUD AND SAY IT PROUD: HELP!

Asking for help is something you need to be willing, and able, to do. I'm sure if you wanted to, you could figure out how to change the oil in your car, and thus save the time it takes to drive to the garage **as** well as the money you spend having someone else do it for you. I bet, though, that you get help when it's time to change your oil, right? Use the same principle when it comes to your business.

Asking for help and seeking out guidance is one of the best ways you can learn to do things yourself. No one is a natural at this kind of thing. It would be almost impossible to be wonderful at everything, and running a business can be overwhelming. Businesses need so much care and feeding! Getting the help you need is the most nurturing thing you can do for your business. You can hire employees, seek out mentors, or join an association or a like-minded group. The options are limitless. The more you're willing to seek out help, the more likely that your options for success will also prove to be limitless.

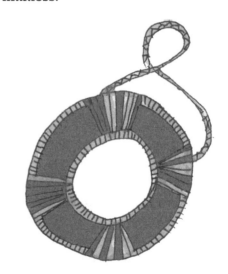

FROM THE CREATIVE COLLECTIVE: MEGAN HUNT

Surround yourself with advisers and mentors who are smarter than you.

MENTORS: YOUR BUSINESS GURUS

Help is out there in many forms. Reading books (thank you!) is a good start, but occasionally you'll need some in-person assistance. We all know that when we're working through something, nothing beats a good cup of coffee or a strong cocktail with a trusted friend. Sometimes, though, even better than a trusted friend is a trusted adviser.

That's where mentors come into play. What *is* a mentor exactly? Simply put, a mentor is someone with extensive experience who wants to see you succeed in your enterprise. They teach you things, they share their secrets and tips and tricks, and they help you understand deals and contracts. You can benefit from their past mistakes, their connections, and their wisdom. A business mentor can offer you guidance, advice, and answers and help you out when you need a contact.

You'll be able to define your relationship with a mentor in a number of different ways. The trick is to seek out a mentor who can help you get to where you want to go and be someone whom you feel you can trust. You can gain a lot from working with someone who has been where you are now, if for no other reason than they can help guide you through situations they've already been through. It is very valuable to have someone on your side who can help you negotiate tricky situations and whose missteps you can learn from. Think of your mentor as a very wise person who not only has been where you are but, most importantly, is also where you want to be.

LOCATING A MENTOR — VIRTUAL AND OTHERWISE

So how do you locate such a magical person? Well, there are nearly as many ways of going about it as there are people to find. Plus, you can have as many mentors as you want. Maybe you need a person who is running a successful business that has a lot in common with yours, or maybe you need a mentor whose footsteps you'd like to follow in.

I happen to have several mentors, but there's a catch. I don't know a single one of them in reality. That's right, my mentors don't even know I exist.

Right now you are either laughing *at* me and thinking I'm nuts or *with* me because you know exactly what I'm talking about. You see, I have chosen a few people whom I admire to use as *virtual* mentors. I do that by studying their history, following their careers, and keeping abreast of what they're up to. I set them as examples for my own path and my own career.

MY TWO MARTHAS

I've mentioned two of my mentors, the first one being Martha Stewart, and the second is Martha Beck. I know I already said that I wouldn't want Martha Stewart's exact life or career because of the yoga-pants-in-the-grocery-store thing, but the real truth is, all joking aside, I like what she has going on. I can also relate to the fact that, like me, Martha S. had several careers before she came to be the woman we know today. She was a model, a stockbroker, and a real-estate agent, but she had a passion for homemaking, cooking, and creating beautiful environments. With her determination and moxie, she turned her passions into a very, *very* successful business.

And look where she has taken those passions! I admire the way her business has so many well-functioning arms: her magazines, her television show, her books, her

I highly suggest having a mentor, someone to help spring ideas off of. Once a month, I meet with a friend who also owns a small business. We meet and discuss our goals for the month, and it's great. It keeps me accountable; otherwise, I have no one to be held accountable to.

interactive website, and her lines of products ranging from paint to furniture, all with her name emblazoned on them. Yep, our Martha does it all! Oh, sure, she has loads of help nowadays. But she started out alone, a one-woman show in her basement kitchen. That kitchen didn't even have refrigerators; she had to depend on the frostiness of her basement to keep her food cold.

So while my big-business dreams aren't the same as Martha Stewart's, we have a lot in common. And I learn a lot from her, and not just how to fold napkins into swans. That makes her a mentor.

Martha Number Two, Martha Beck, the life coach, is a mentor to me in different ways. I respond to the way she thinks and writes. Her methods for digging deep and solving problems work for me. I use the advice she gives to help me improve my own life both personally and professionally.

From Martha B., I've learned more about my goals and intentions, and for that I'll be forever grateful. I've read all her books, many of which I've downloaded to listen to in my car. While we've never met in person, she and her wisdom have accompanied me on long road trips, and more than once she has advised me before a big meeting or when I'm negotiating a contract or designing a class. She's also the wise woman we can thank for that "beginning at the end" exercise we did a few pages ago.

IN-PERSON MENTORS

The other kind of mentor, of course, is the kind you actually know or get to know in real life. An in-person mentor is a wonderful thing. It is amazing to be able to meet one-on-one with someone who has wonderful ideas and advice to share and will open up your eyes to new opportunities. This mentor — most likely a local person — can be another business owner whom you meet with as often as it works and is convenient for the both of you. And, of course, nowadays you don't need to have actual face-to-face meetings. You can Skype with them (video conferencing over the Internet), and you can develop a hearty email relationship.

Most businesspeople have sought out mentoring themselves at one point or another, so they're really open-minded about helping others who are just getting started.

Look around your town or your community, find someone whose business you admire, and then ask them out for coffee and make your pitch! In the United States, you can also find mentors through programs like SCORE or the Small Business Administration (SBA). Also check out your local chamber of commerce. Attending their mixers and other events is a great way to meet like-minded business leaders and connect with them on a professional level.

If the business you want or have isn't the chamber-of-commerce-membership kind, no worries. The creative community is so open and giving, chances are, if you know someone, even if it's just online, who would be a good match for you, go for it. Just because someone doesn't live nearby or even in the same country doesn't mean that they won't be willing to help you if they're interested.

However you and your mentor end up finding each other, choose to work together in a way that is satisfactory to both of you and creates that all-important sense of trust, which is, of course, a two-way street.

MENTOR MATCH-UP

So how do you decide who would be a good mentor for you? Look at the people you admire. Pay attention to what it is you like about someone else. Do you like the direction their career has taken? Do you admire their business model? The opportunities they have or have acted on? The way they seem to balance their business and personal lives? Do the two of you share a similar beginning?

Reaching out to a mentor isn't as intimidating as it may initially sound, but before you do, get a clear picture of the kind of relationship you want. What is it you hope to gain from a relationship with a mentor? What would be your ideal session with them? What is it exactly that you'd like to learn from them?

And what will the mentor get from your relationship? What is the benefit for them?

EXERCISE
Get out your trusty journal and compile a list of qualities you'd like to find in a mentor. Compassion? Understanding? Creativity? Does your ideal mentor have smashing creative skills? Are they known for their big customer base or their ability to develop new programs and products? Is their website super-duper and inventive? Then compile a second list, this one detailing what you can offer a mentor. Make a list of qualities and services you can offer your prospective guru.

TO PAY OR NOT

This brings us around to the point that if you choose to do so, you can pay for mentoring. Lots of people out there who are wonderful mentors do it for a living. If you decide to work with a fee-based mentor, first do a lot of research. You need to take a really hard look at what they are offering and what they promise you'll get from working with them. Then you need to follow up with their former students and read all of their testimonials. Most likely they have a few products, like courses or books, for sale. Make the investment in one of them to check out their style. Do you respond well to the way they explain things or teach? Do they just seem to get you? Perfect! If you don't respond well to their products (or free offerings if they're available), chances are you won't respond well to their other services, so if you can, take 'em for a test drive.

A lot of people think that if you pay for your mentor relationship, you'll get more value from it. This is based on the assumption that if one pays for something, one is more likely to take full advantage of the experience and work harder, to boot. I tend to think this is true, but I don't think it's the only way to have a successful relationship with a mentor.

How someone can benefit from mentoring you (other than financially) depends on what you can bring to the table. In exchange for their expert advice, you could perhaps do some research for them, help with their books, or polish up their web copy. Bartering for services is sometimes welcome, and if money is tight and your mentor is open to it, put together a package of goods or services that they won't want to turn down.

Remember, you're askin', wishin', and a-hopin' that they will open up their vault of genius and let you in. You can really benefit from lessons they've already learned, contacts they've already made, and paths they've already forged. Make it a mutually beneficial relationship.

EXERCISE

Imagine meeting with a mentor for the first time. What would you want to discuss during your time with them? What questions would you ask about their business? What do they have now that you hope they can help you get?

FAULTY FIT

If you wind up (sadly) connecting with a mentor who turns out to be a bad fit for you, don't worry. Just politely and professionally cut your losses and find someone new. Like everything else in life, sometimes things just don't work. You don't click with everyone you meet in your personal life, and your business life is the same way.

When I was thinking of opening that cupcakery way back when, I had a mentor, a very friendly gentleman from a professional business organization. I was matched up with him because he had owned several successful eateries. When he decided to retire from the food business, he generously devoted some of his newfound free time to working with young people like me.

Let's call him Mr. Doubt. Mr. Doubt and I met for about an hour each week over the course of six weeks. I was to share my business plan with him and benefit from his good advice. He was really very kind to me, but in the end, we had to break up.

Why? Because he thought the concept of a bakery that only sold one item was a terrible, awful, horrendous idea. Mr. Doubt could not wrap his mind around the idea of a cupcakery. Mr. Doubt tried to convince me to make wedding cakes or even chocolate chip cookies if I was insistent on focusing on one kind of baked good. But *cupcakes*? No way could he get behind that. We went around and around about the very thing that I wanted to do the most.

Mr. Doubt and I simply could not meet in the middle, and after awhile it was obvious that we were not going to work well together. He told me time and time again that the world did not want to embrace the concept of cupcakes as a luxury dessert item. He was very clear that cupcakes were only for children's birthday parties and not for grown-ups. He thought cupcakes were ridiculous, and because I was so gung-ho about cupcakes, he tended to think that I was ridiculous, too.

We parted on friendly terms even though in the end he laughed me off. He said he felt bad for me for having such a limited imagination and that he was positive I would end up brokenhearted because (a) no one was going to loan me money for a cupcake business, and (b) I would never have any customers.

Well, Mr. Doubt, I'm raising a vegan cupcake in your honor all these years later. While I may not have opened that specialty bakery, I sure do patronize them every chance I get. National cupcake chains are now huge, and for a while cupcakes were even more popular than traditional wedding cakes for those super-special events. I'm pretty sure I would have had a successful cupcakery had I continued with my venture, but not if I had listened to that one mentor who just didn't share my vision.

Lesson to be learned: It always pays to follow your own heart.

EXERCISE

Working with other people in this way can be really exciting. It is really empowering to share your hopes, dreams, fears, and concerns with folks who really get where you're coming from. Trusting people, including strangers, which some of these people may well be at first, is a personal choice. They must be something special, though, or else you wouldn't have wanted to connect with them so closely in the first place, right? The more open and forthcoming you are about where your business is and what your skills are, the better off you'll be.

Take out your journal and work on these questions:

- What areas of my business could I use some help with?
- Who has a business that's like the 2.0 or even the 4.0 version of my own?
- Whose business do I really admire?
- How would I best like to work with a mentor?
- What would my ideal relationship with a mentor look like?
- What can I offer in return?

FROM THE CREATIVE COLLECTIVE: ABBY KERR

One of the biggest benefits of working with a mentor is the privilege of her perspective. Having been further down the road than you in your industry, she can see patterns and dynamics you can't and make predictions you aren't able to. She can assure you that what you're experiencing is normal for your phase of business growth.

Miz Alex Franzen works with some of the most sought-after mentors in the coaching world. She has the inside track on how these relationships are formed, how they work, and how they can do both parties justice.

Mentors. We all need 'em, and someday most of us hope to be one. What are some creative, honest, authentic ways that we can use to approach people we want to get to know better? If someone turns down our heartfelt request, how can we respond gracefully? And what should we be looking for in a mentor?

Approaching a potential mentor is a strategic art, as is the act of mentoring itself. Mentorees, you've got to court your would-be mentor like a Victorian gentleman or lady: elegantly, respectfully, and with an appropriate sense of pacing. And mentors, you've got to wrangle your pro bono commitments with grace or risk sinking into loathsome resentment. Which serves no one. 'Specially you.

What is your best advice for mentorees?

Introduce yourself to your desired mentor with a simple email. Write as a peer, not a frothy-mouthed fan (even if secretly you are one). Keep it concise; brevity is respectful. Two or three short paragraphs, max. Their time is valuable, as is your own.

Reference a specific way in which this person has already positively influenced your life. Did their last book blow your circuits? Do you hang on their every tweet? Do you refresh your browser every hour, salivating over their next blog entry? Let your enthusiasm shine with specificity. If you've already invested in their empire by purchasing their products, attending their events, or signing up for their e-course, remind them.

Express a desire to support them, and offer a few concrete things you might be able to assist with, free of charge. Establish a relationship anchored on reciprocity and generosity from the get-go. Position yourself as a useful apprentice.

Very, very important: I'd recommend *not* asking for a mentorship relationship outright during your first interaction with your would-be mentor. That's a bit like cramming your tongue down someone's throat at the beginning of your very first date. Uncool. And kinda revolting. Wait for a reply, gauge the recipient's interest level, and *then* make your request, after you've treated them to lunch, mailed them a gift from their Amazon Wish List, or sent a few clients their way. Reciprocity. It really works!

If the object of your mentorship affection turns down your request, do not whine, plead, or challenge their decision. Bow, nod, and stride off with your head held high. It's gotta be *Game On!* for both parties, or it's a no-go.

What is your best advice for mentors?

When you're approached by a prospective mentoree, resist the urge to blurt out, "Yes, yes, a thousand times, yes!" without a moment's hesitation. It's fantastic to be sought after. And fan mail is flattering. But let yourself sleep on it, assess your schedule, check your gut, cross a few Ts, and then make an informed decision.

Clear boundaries will make the difference between an elegant relationship and a goopy mudslide. From day one, create a firm container for your mentoring relationship by getting all the logistics squared away. For example:

» Is this is a strictly pro bono situation?
» Is there a barter component?
» Is this a one-time-only hour of goodwill consulting, or will you be connecting on a recurring basis?
» Will you be meeting in person or virtually? Skype or phone?
» What's the duration of your commitment?
» What's your mentoree's central concern, need, or goal?

If your mentoree is cluttering your inbox with endless requests and questions, gently (but firmly) ask them to pack up their exuberance till it's time for your next scheduled meet-up. Don't establish a pattern of replying to each missive on the spot. Not that you would. But truly . . . don't.

If you feel your mentoree would be better served by professional coaching, business consulting, academic training, hands-on Reiki, psychotherapy, or whatever else, tell them. You are not responsible for soothing every inflammation that filters into your inbox. Honesty is humane, and heroically potent.

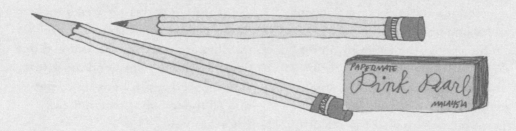

YOUR PERSONAL BOARD OF DIRECTORS

Another way to go about finding help for your business, not only as a profit-generating machine but also for yourself as a businessperson, is to develop a board of directors.

Most for-profit and not-for profit businesses have boards of directors to oversee the activities of a company. Basically, the board keeps tabs on the way the company is run. These groups of people get together and solve problems, suggest ideas and solutions, and make sure that everything is running smoothly. Some of them bring certain skill sets to the boardroom meeting table, and some members may have a personal or financial stake in making sure the company does well.

I have personally volunteered on many not-for-profit boards, and instead of making a monetary contribution to their bottom line, I've offered my services in kind if I just didn't have the extra cash. I have handled public relations and marketing duties as my role in helping these organizations thrive. Volunteering like this has taught me many valuable business lessons and has made me feel like a real member of my community.

Now, your business may not need to assemble a board of experts to decide on every single thing you do, but you can still benefit from the concept because, let's face it, we can all profit from advice and a solid sounding board now and again.

KEY POSITIONS

Assembling a board of directors works sort of the same way as finding a mentor does. You don't have to know all of your board members to benefit from their wisdom. Decide what kind of help you seek most, and then fill the jobs! To get you started, here are a couple of key positions you can consider for your very own personal board of directors.

MONEY PERSON

Look for a financial guru who speaks in a way that you understand, someone you really dig. There are lots of money and finance people to choose from. You can find them online, from books, and through referrals.

MARKETING PERSON

Seek out someone with marketing experience that your company can benefit from. This person should give good advice, have solid examples that will work for you, and be accessible. At the very least, this person should set good, workable examples that you can follow.

BIG THINKER

What I mean by this is *find someone you know who thinks big.* This person should be able to look at your overall concepts and business plan and see where you have holes, and then help you fix them. This person should help you leave your comfort zone and expand your horizons.

MISCELLANEOUS GURUS

You may also want to find people who are experts in web commerce, web design, blogging, and public relations.

GIVE AND TAKE

If you know your board members in real life, you can ask to meet with them as a group or individually once a month. During your time together, make sure you're taking full advantage of what your members have to offer.

Ask your board members to give you advice, recommend books, and refer you to other types of resources like contacts, clients, vendors, and even courses they think you and your business could benefit from.

This is another situation where you want to give back as much as you get. Find some way to add benefit to your board members' lives. One way to give back is to remember how wonderful these resources have been for you, and when you're in the position to be on someone else's board of directors or mentor someone like yourself, jump at the chance. (Yes, pay it forward!)

OK. Let's face it. It might be really tough for you to find a real-life person who fits each of these roles that you can talk to, let alone meet with, once a month or even once a quarter. And if you *could* find them, you might feel silly bringing them all together just to focus on you. Just because it works for some, doesn't mean it will work for everyone. So just as you can have a virtual mentor, you can also have a virtual board of directors.

Find online board members and simply set aside time in your calendar to check in with them. If you do your books the second Tuesday of each month, add some time in your calendar on that day to catch up with virtual money people you like. You don't have to follow their blogs or see what they're up to each day; just add them into your normal bookkeeping routine. If you learn something helpful or new from them that month, send along a little message, letting them know that you appreciate what they wrote or a tool they introduced. Everyone likes to know that what they're doing is working, so if you benefit from their advice or products, make sure they know you appreciate it.

These kinds of relationships will be so beneficial that occasionally you might find them overwhelming.

Take some time each week or once a month to review what you've learned, and find ways to apply these lessons to your business. You should be getting lots of hot tips and ideas to plug into your business plan.

Running your business won't always just be a cycle of creating / posting / social media / marketing / selling / books / begin again. Taking the time to really absorb and implement what you're taking away from your business relationships is paramount.

Make a list of all the different areas in your business. Now, to get started finding mentors or board members for yourself, turn to your favorite social-media website. You'll be able to easily find experts in all the areas where you need some additional guidance. Subscribe to their feeds and set some time aside to review the messages they're putting out to the world. Take notes while you're reading what they say. Follow up on their links and investigate people or resources that they recommend. Hopefully you'll find a few gems.

BUILD A BRAIN TRUST

At some point when I began my consulting and coaching business, it became clear to me that I couldn't do it alone. One of the things I missed most about working for someone else was having coworkers. You know what I mean, right? People whom I could complain to, with whom I could brainstorm, vent frustrations, eat lunch, and share my achievements.

People who got what my work life was like because they were in it with me.

When I realized that this important social component was missing from my own business, I set out to re-create it. I wanted to connect with other writers, coaches, and businesswomen who also worked alone at home.

I emailed and Skyped with several women I thought would fit the bill. I shared with them my business highs and lows and told them that I was looking for a safe place to connect with people who were going through the same sorts of struggles and challenges that I was. What resulted was a Brain Trust.

We built ourselves a private online meeting place (we use Google Groups), and we meet there whenever we need to. This kind of business support has been amazing for me. While our group shares some of the same qualities that a personal board of directors or a mentor relationship would, we mostly just support each other. Having people who can cheer you on and occasionally cheer you up is an excellent business resource.

We practice marketing pitches on each other, review price structures, pass on media leads, talk about new ideas, and pretty much do what a good in-person coworker would do for you if you had one.

I love my little online Brain Trust and couldn't do half of what I do without them.

STREET TEAMS AND PROFESSIONAL ASSOCIATIONS

Don't overlook the possibility of help and support that you can get from local or national associations or even street teams. For those unfamiliar with the term, a *street team* is a marketing term for a group of people who hit the streets promoting an event or a product. Street teams have become a standard and highly effective promotional tool used by corporations, media outfits, entertainment companies, and many other industries that market to consumers.

Does your area of expertise have a national association or a local chapter that you can join? If so, this can be a wonderful resource for you. Do a quick search on the Internet and see what you turn up. Be sure to look at these groups closely. Do they have fees or dues? A regular meeting day? If you find a group you're curious about, write to them and ask for the name of a member whom you can get in touch with, and then do some research.

Every single drab business book you pick up or boring business class you take will talk to you about developing an elevator speech. "Describe your business in just a few sentences. Blah blah blah. . . ." And while you're at it, make it sound intriguing enough to start a conversation about what you do, to drum up business, or to just plain impress the pants off the person you're talking to. Sounds tough, huh? Well, I'll admit it can be a challenge to make magic with just a couple of sentences, but a very savvy member of my Creative Collective will show you just how.

Michelle, you're a real pro at elevator speeches. Can you tell us when it's a good time to use one?
Ooh, lots of times and places! Whenever someone asks you The Dreaded Question: "So...what do you do?" And, of course, on your website / Etsy shop / Facebook page / Twitter bio...basically, all over the Interwebs.

What key elements should an elevator speech have?
I think the answer to that goes back to how elevator speeches got their name. Back in the day, the only way to communicate your Big Idea to the president of the company (I picture him being stoic, with a mustache and a cigar and a curvy blonde always on his arm) was to hope you wound up in the elevator with him. So you needed to have your pitch at the ready, and it needed to take under 15 seconds to hook the boss into green lighting your idea then and there, or about the amount of time it would take to get from an upper floor of the building down to the lobby. Or at least to ask the curvy blonde on his arm to set up

a meeting with you (obviously we're in an episode of *Mad Men* in this scenario).

It's all about being articulate, concise, and intriguing in about three sentences or less. (Don't I make it sound easy?)

Any words of wisdom for making sure one's speech is fresh and original? You don't want to sound like a recording of yourself or be dumbstruck into saying the same thing over and over.
Firstly, it should answer the following questions about your business:

» Why do you rock people's socks?
» Why are you doing what you do, in terms of your business?
» Why do you think you can succeed in your business?
» What do you want to be known for in your business?
» Why do you care about your field?
» What difference do you want to make in your field?

Then go over what you wrote in your journal, and pull out the articulate/concise/intriguing stuff. If that's too difficult, answer each question in one sentence based on what you wrote for the answer. Once that's done, write down your answer to the "So…what do you do?" Dreaded Question and say it out loud. Are there any words there that read well but don't sound natural coming out of your mouth? Rewrite it until you would feel comfortable saying to a stranger what's written on the page.

After that, it's practice, practice, practice! Saying it out loud to the mirror counts, but saying it to your loved ones (who won't think you're weird or crazy or want to knock you down or run away) is even better. It's not about memorizing it so that you say it in the same way to each person you meet from now until the end of time, but it's about being comfortable and confident and articulate with your answer.

How can someone pitch their skills and business without sounding like a big slice of processed cheese?
I have to reiterate that this isn't your "forever and ever" elevator speech. Instead, this is what you commit to saying *now* when you meet someone new and get asked The Dreaded Question or put on your Twitter bio,

et cetera. Your pitch is supposed to be fluid and change and grow, along with the increased clarity you get regarding your products, services, and niche.

Because of that, you'll find that the key in tweaking your elevator speech for the better is to pay attention to the feedback you get when you say it out in the world. When does someone lean in to hear more or otherwise express interest with their body language? What follow-up questions do they ask? Originally, I didn't have, "I'm the When I Grow Up Coach" in my pitch. Instead, I'd call myself "a certified life coach" or a "creative-career coach." It was only when I was in a group Firestarter session with Danielle LaPorte (love her!) where I introduced myself as the When I Grow Up Coach, and only because I knew that she knew me that way! I was shocked when the room of 20+ women laughed and leaned in, waiting to hear more as to what that meant. I knew I'd be an idiot to not include that in my introduction from now on, and it's stuck.

Also, revisiting the questions can keep things fresh and new. If your answers don't change every few months, be concerned that things are stagnant or stale in your biz.

Can you give us a little sample of your own elevator speech?
Sure! Mine is simply: "I'm the When I Grow Up Coach! I help creative types devise the career they think they can't have, or discover it to begin with!"

Part 2

PLANNING
FOR SUCCESS

Chapter 8

TYPES OF BUSINESS MODELS

Now that you've gained insight and clarity as to why (and what) you want to be in business for, it's time to get down to brass tacks, or nuts and bolts, or whatever other hardware analogy you might wish to use to conjure up the components of your enterprise from which you can produce a workable business plan. For starters, you need to determine your business model.

BUSINESS MODEL DEFINED

Business model is a term used to describe how a business is run. It involves everything from how and where the work is done, the methods used to reach customers, and how revenue is brought in. A business model is sort of like an overview of a business, whereas a business plan is more detailed and can include studies, projections, and a thousand other details about the business itself.

Business models come in all shapes and sizes. In fact, these days the sky seems to be the limit when it comes to how you set up your business. For example, a fast-food restaurant franchise is one kind of model, and your local big-box home-goods store is another. An online store is yet another example of a business model — and so are a home-based design office and a food truck that drives around your city selling waffles. These businesses all have vastly different ways of getting their products to the consumer. Deciding on what kind of business model will work best for you is an important part of your business plan. For starters, where and how you sell your product affects a lot of what you're going to do. If your dream is to open your own storefront, but you need to work toward that, you have a good place to start. If you plan on manufacturing something and will need a place to store and ship products from, you need to plan for *that* kind of space. If your business is just getting off the ground, you may have to convince

FROM THE CREATIVE COLLECTIVE: JOLIE GUILLEBEAU

Incorporate your business into your life in whatever way it fits for you. Don't feel like you have to use someone else's model, just because that worked for them. Make it your own and it will flow seamlessly into the other parts of your life.

your partner in life or business (or both) that taking it up a notch is a good idea. (Hello, business plan!)

Let's explore some of the most common options.

RUNNING YOUR BUSINESS FROM HOME

Whether it is economics or personal preference that keeps your business in the home, being home-based is a pretty common choice. Lots and lots of people work from their homes and have wonderful success. Of course, how you're able to make this scenario work depends on what your business is. Naturally it's much easier to set up a home office in a spare room, basement, garage, or even in some cases a walk-in closet if your work mostly involves a computer and a small desk or worktable.

WILL IT WORK OR WON'T IT?

Running your company from home can be a really positive experience, but it can also come with its own set of challenges. You'll need to take careful stock of your life to decide if it'll work. Later in the process of planning your business, you'll have many other details to consider, but let's just look at what you have to deal with for starters:

Do you have a physical area to set up shop? If the answer is yes, does the space have enough room to hold everything you need in one place? Can you install things like a phone line or an Internet connection if you need them in this space? Do you have the ability to store all of your materials and supplies here?

Does your home provide you with the emotional space you need to run your business? What I mean by this is, will you have the actual creative space you need to get your work done? Anyone who has even tried to work from home knows that the distractions you'll face are limitless. From the dogs needing to be walked or dropping their toys at your feet every 10 minutes, to your parents calling to check in, to kids needing your attention, to the pile of dirty laundry that's calling out to you, to looking out the window and realizing that the lawn desperately needs mowing. And, hey, if you suddenly get stuck in your creative process, it can seem like the ideal time to go scrub the bathroom with a toothbrush!

BENEFITS

On the flip side, the benefits of running your company from home can be the same as the downsides. You can be with your pets all day. You're around more for your kids and available when your mom wants to chat. The laundry gets washed and put away because you're around to do it. And letting your mind wander freely while mowing the lawn (it's a very Zen experience) might lead you to the perfect idea for a client. Indeed, along with all those other little responsibilities, your bathroom may never be cleaner because you're home to attend to that soap-scummy bathtub.

SPACE CONSIDERATIONS

If you decide that working from home is what's best for you and your business, great! But you'll need to set up some guidelines to keep yourself on track. (I did it for years, although I am sorry to say that never once when I was stuck did I ever clean my bathroom with a toothbrush.) First of all, make sure your designated space is very clearly set up for your business, with everything you need in that one area. This will not only help you separate your work life from your home life, but also you'll have what you need at hand, allowing you to really focus when you're in that space. It's no good to have to leave your work to go hunt down a particular supply or find the phone when you need to call a client.

If you live with other people, it's important to set up boundaries with them. Maybe post your office hours on the door of your space, and explain that when you're in your workspace during those hours, you're off limits.

DRESS FOR SUCCESS

Are you having trouble staying focused in your sweet home office or studio space?

Look down. Are you wearing your pajamas? If so, get thee to thy closet and put on what you would be wearing if you were heading out to a "professional" day job.

My official personal studies of my own work habits show that if I approach my workday in my PJs and cozy slippers, my productivity is on par with my outfit. Here's the bummer of that: Lots of us want to work for ourselves because we want complete freedom, and that includes freedom of wardrobe choices. In fact, one of my primary motivations to work for myself is because I never wanted to wear stuffy, office-appropriate clothes again. The thought of staying in comfy clothes and never again wearing painful high heels is very appealing to me. However, the old saying that you must dress for success has some truth to it.

Making sure that you're dressed and groomed before you begin your workday can go a long way toward ensuring that you get your work done. In fact, a trick I use on myself quite often, one that people really respond to when I talk about it in classes I teach or speeches and talks I give, is this: when I'm on a tight deadline or really need to get going on a project, I put on my highest red heels. This tortuous pair of shoes is a holdover from my days as 9-to-5 marketing person. These were my power shoes: four-inch heels, pointy toes, and beautiful stitching. I used to wear them when I needed extra confidence, and I couldn't wear them for very long. I would carry them in my bag and put them on right before going into a big meeting and remove them as soon as I could. Oh, how they hurt! But they kept me focused, and their magic still works to this day. Once those bad boys go on my feet, I'm so anxious to get them off that I stay focused on the task at hand and get down to business.

WORKING STYLE

Another hamper to productivity is being too cozy. If you snuggle up on your comfy, squishy sofa and put a blanket across your lap and allow your pets or kids to cuddle up next to you, and you have a mug of yummy tea or coffee right next you, are you intending to get your work done or to relax with a good book? Sending mixed signals to your brain about what you should be doing (your financial records for the past month) and what it seems like you're telling your body to do (relax!) can be a hard trap to get out of. If you work like this but find you're having trouble staying on task, change you're style and see if it makes a difference.

Also, try to learn what parts of your business *can* be conducted in such a casual way. Perhaps you're able to catch up on design blogs that are relevant to your business or source new supplies from the comfort of your bed or couch while your accounting details, customer correspondence, and website updating are best done from a more structured place.

RENTING A STUDIO OR OFFICE

Renting a place to work is an option that many creative people chose. In fact, it's what I do. I rent studio space in an old mill building in the next town over from me. And just as with working from home, there are upsides and downsides.

UPSIDES

The biggest upside I've found (and perhaps you can relate to this) is my frame of mind. It's far easier for me to focus on the task at hand when I'm at my studio. Having fewer distractions allows me to get into a working mindset as does the fact that I actually have to leave my house to accomplish that work. This means doing things that often didn't happen when I worked from home, like getting dressed every day. Seriously! When I worked from home, there were entire days when I stayed in my pajamas, which was a part of my dream of working for myself. Once I get to the mill building and climb the four flights of stairs to my 250-square-foot studio, I'm ready to work. That is a big improvement over how I felt when I worked at home.

Another major benefit is that I can see clients in my studio if I need to. During my work-at-home phase, I never met clients at my house. I held meetings in coffee shops, the local

FROM THE CREATIVE COLLECTIVE: MEGAN HUNT

What I love about coworking is that we tend to work harder when we are surrounded by people who are also on task. There are fewer distractions, and we feel motivated by the productive atmosphere. But unlike working at home or in a coffee shop, the downtime is also more productive. Side conversations become collaborations, distractions become fun new inside jokes, and getting up to stretch becomes riding a Razor scooter down the hallway. A day at the office for us includes relaxing on a comfy couch with a laptop, good coffee, a muffin from a local bakery, and maybe even a beer, and being motivated and inspired by all of the productivity, fun, and camaraderie surrounding us. A recent Gallup study showed that the happiest people get eight hours of social interaction every day. We have trouble finding time to be social when we are always working, but why can't we mix the two? Coworking actually has helped me out a lot because being around the positive energy of other hardworking people tends to validate my own efforts and motivate me to press on.

park, and even my local library. Now it's easier than ever to work with people one-on-one. Plus, I just feel more professional.

For people whose work can be noisy (say, a woodworker) or if you're someone who likes to crank the music up when you work, an off-site studio or office can be a lifesaver. It's much easier to use a saw in a commercial studio than it is in your home.

DOWNSIDES

Downsides can be plentiful, too, of course. You may not like your

neighbors, and they may play their music too loudly for *your* taste. It's possible that you can afford the rent but not the means to fix up the space right away. You'll have more bills, of course (more on that coming up), which you have to be ready for. Plus, you have to make the effort to get to that studio or office — even in winter snow or when you just plain don't feel like it.

AN OPTION

Coworking is a type of space arrangement that is gaining popularity. Here, you simply share your space and some of the duties that go along with the space. For example, you might share your space with another knitwear designer, and you would split the bills and possibly the cost of a yarn winder or some software and the copier as well as the cleaning duties.

RENTING A STOREFRONT AND KEEPING SHOP HOURS

Renting a store and setting up a space to receive the public is very, very exciting. The best job I ever had before I became a full-time writer was managing a retail store. It was a very small home-goods shop, and the woman who owned it was my mentor. I had lots of freedom there, and I thrived. This is not to say that it wasn't a lot of hard work, because believe me, running that store was the hardest job I've ever had, and I've had lots of hard jobs. But there was no better feeling than a shop full of customers, a ringing cash register, and the satisfaction of a successful day.

CHALLENGES AND REWARDS

The hard parts were keeping the store looking amazing and fresh, getting customers in the door, and selling enough stock to keep up with all the costs that factored into running a store. If I was sick, I had to go in to work. If there was a big storm, I had to be at the shop. I had to travel to buy inventory, and that took me away from home. There were days when I had no paying customers. None.

FROM THE CREATIVE COLLECTIVE: **SUE EGGEN**

I took the advice of my father, who said, "For your business to grow, you need a bigger space." He was right! Giant Dwarf operated full-time out of a 10-by-10 room in my apartment, with an assistant, an intern, a fiancé, and two cats. We were constantly shifting projects from table space to table space, which was extremely time consuming and frustrating. The bigger the company grew, the less space we had to work in. It was clearly time to get out of there and into a bigger studio.

I couldn't afford full-time help, so I had two very part-time employees. Depending on them was occasionally tough, too, because like me they got sick sometimes, but unlike me, they could call in sick, a luxury I couldn't afford for myself.

I had to always be "on" when someone came in, which was tough for me. Just like running an online business, customers were sometimes thrilled and sometimes . . . they were not. I had to have lots of policies in place for returns and exchanges. I had to have an advance plan of what to do if someone wanted to ship his or her purchases or if someone broke something in the shop. I had to design and execute attractive, enticing window displays; keep up with trends in the world of home goods; and deal with solicitors. Plus, I had to find time to interact with the local business community, decide how to handle charity requests, and not only learn the most advantageous places to advertise but also figure out how to pay for those ads.

The challenges of owning a little store (or in my case, working for someone who owned a little store) are many. However, if that is where your heart is, and if you decide that it's the best thing for your business, it can be really rewarding. You must be ready to have two jobs. Your first job is managing the store, which includes dealing with vendors, insurance agents, landlords, and employees (if you have them), and your second job is stocking or creating what you plan to sell.

Be prepared to put in many, many hours and know how to plunge a toilet yourself, because plumbers aren't free.

When I first met Jessie, she was working for a company that had a booth at the New York Gift Show, and I ordered her then-company's products for my store. We kept in touch over the years, and I was thrilled when she eventually followed her heart and left her full-time gig to open her own gallery and pursue her art. Not only is she an incredibly talented artist, creating fun work, but she now owns her own brick-and-mortar business in Seattle, where I've since traveled to do a book signing, so I got to see her gallery for myself.

Jessie, how did you make the leap from corporate job to gallery owner?

It was actually a fairly organic transition. I started my blog in 2007, and as a result of reader requests, I began selling original artwork, prints, and note cards based on my artwork featured on the site via Etsy later that same year. By 2008, the sales had grown to the point where I was able to cut down my day job to part-time [and devote more time to my business]. Then sales increased sufficiently so that I had enough confidence to quit my day job entirely. After a few years as a freelancer, the owners of a local gallery where I sold artwork announced that they wanted to sell as they were having a baby and wanted to switch to a home-based business; I felt like I was ready to move on to the next step, and it felt like a good natural transition. The store has led to a variety of great opportunities and increased my visibility so much.

If someone is interested in opening their own brick-and-mortar shop, what's your top advice?

Prepare yourself for some very long hours, make sure you have comfortable shoes, and psych yourself up daily because you're going to have to smile even when you don't want to sometimes and hear the same questions over and over. It can be hard to stay "on" all day! Also, forget about socializing during the Christmas season. You will be working.

Did you have to share your business plan with anyone, like your landlord? If so, what was the reaction?

I did have to pitch myself to my landlord, who was dubious based on checking out my online store and looking at my website. But after meeting with him in person, somehow I made him a believer.

Do you have any advice when folks are looking for vendors or suppliers?

Seek out other businesses in your area, and ask for advice. I have had great luck doing this. Also, you'd be amazed at how much you can find by crowd-sourcing on Twitter and Facebook, or simply asking other business owners who produce things you admire.

THE OFF-SITE BOTTOM LINE

There are obvious reasons why renting a studio or retail space can be tough, but these types of challenges can be overcome, provided you're willing to work at them.

The biggest and most obvious challenge is financial. You'll need money to rent a space, and most likely a lot of it. You have to think about escrow deposits, utilities, insurance, furnishing your space, licenses, and whatever else your state or local officials require you to have. Not to worry, though. If that's what your heart is set on, a business plan will help you see all of the possibilities ahead of you.

Here are some things to think about and notate in your journal:

➤➤ What kind of space is best for you right now?

➤➤ What kind of space would you have in a perfect world?

➤➤ What are your needs from your space? Do you have to see clients, host trunk shows, or often make a big mess?

➤➤ What is your budget for a space?

➤➤ Would you be comfortable sharing a space with another business owner?

➤➤ Where are the best locations or opportunities for you in your area?

➤➤ What do you already have on hand to furnish a workspace?

➤➤ What would the benefits be to you and your family?

EXERCISE

In your journal, make a pros-and-cons list, detailing the benefits and downsides of where you run your business now and the potential benefits (and downsides) if you ran your business from another location.

Brainstorm a bit in your journal. What does your ideal business model look like? Write up a description that includes how and where you would like to conduct your business. What does your perfect setting look like? How do you serve your clients and customers from this space?

Jennifer Lee is one of my favorite creative-business resources of all time. When I first learned of her concept for creative-business planning, called The Right-Brain Business Plan, I was smitten. She helps creative folk who respond to things visually better than they may respond to charts, facts, and figures design and explore what their business values and paths may look like. By using her creative method for business planning, which involves a lot of hands-on fun and crafty work, people often find hidden surprises in their hopes and dreams that help them to get on the right path to make their business visions come true.

You developed a wonderful process called The Right-Brain Business Plan. This has turned into successful e-courses, an online community, and a best-selling book of the same name. What kind of person could benefit most from looking at their business with their "right brain"?

Creative entrepreneurs who have a passion for their work but loathe the left-brain details, like marketing plans or numbers-related tasks, would benefit most from looking at their business with their right brain. What many creative entrepreneurs don't realize is that their creativity is their most valuable business asset. By tapping into their right-brain genius, they can come up with new, innovative ideas that can set them apart from the crowd.

What is your favorite business-planning tip?

My favorite business-planning tip is using my sticky note project plan. I tack up large wall calendars in my creative space and use colored sticky notes to map out all of my milestones and to-dos over several months. It keeps my projects top of mind, helps me plan out my workload, and allows me to easily track my progress.

Once you started practicing your idea of right-brain business planning, what were the effects on your own business?
I made my first Right-Brain Business Plan at my kitchen table in November 2007. The following year, I doubled my income, reached my target number of coaching clients, led workshops regularly, appeared on television twice, and launched two products. I also included a handmade book on my first Right-Brain Business Plan because I had a goal to write a book. I'm happy to say that that little book is now part of the artwork on the cover of my actual book, *The Right-Brain Business Plan.*

Have you made any big mistakes in running your business? If so, what did you take away from the experience that helped your business become stronger?
One of the biggest mistakes I made was trying to do everything myself for too long. For example, I waited until my accounting system was a disaster and I had already wasted hours of precious time trying to reconcile my books before I hired a bookkeeper to fix my mess. Now I just send off my receipts and statements to my bookkeeper and get to spend my time on my work and passion. I'm learning to delegate more so that I can focus on big-picture thinking and more revenue-generating activities.

Chapter 9

BUSINESS PLAN PRELIMINARIES

Even after deciding not to pursue my cupcake business, I held on to the dream for a long time, partly because my business plan had ignited a fire in my soul for being my own boss, and, most importantly, for doing something that made me crazy, over-the-moon happy. So while the initial impetus and idea went nowhere, those core realizations that I took from my planning were invaluable, and for that I'm grateful.

WHAT IS A BUSINESS PLAN, AND WHY DO YOU NEED ONE?

Writing your business plan does not have to be all consuming. I encourage you to work on it when you have not only the time but also the desire. If you only choose to make part of a plan, that's OK. Obviously if you need to focus on one area, like budgeting or marketing, you'll be motivated to dig into those sections. Conversely, if working out the finer details of your money is as about as appealing as sitting in a math class for the rest of your life, perhaps it's best to skip it until your ready to tackle that reality. (Keep in mind that the business plan you create for yourself can be a bit different than the plan you would need to provide to a bank when applying for a loan. Numbers may not be your thing, but you will have to get them in order to talk to a bank.)

The point is, write it at your own pace and do what seems right to you. When getting started with a brand-new business plan, work on it where it feels the most comfortable. If you're computer oriented, great; if you happen to be more of a pen-and-paper person, that'll work, too. The point is to put the plan together in the most effective way for the purpose you have in mind.

THERE IS NO WRONG WAY TO WRITE A PLAN

Remember: There is no wrong way. You are not going to make any life-altering mistakes. And even if you

FROM THE CREATIVE COLLECTIVE: LISA CONGDON

I think about my business plan almost every day. I am one of those really goal-oriented people, so I'm almost always thinking about where I am today in relationship to where I want to be tomorrow.

do, there will always be a chance to correct them. Creating a business plan can feel so *final*. The act of outlining your business on paper may feel limiting: What if you change your mind about something? What if something doesn't work out? What if you can't do the math or express yourself in a clear way?

Those are valid fears and concerns, sure, but you don't need to worry your pretty little business head about them.

Your business plan is a living, breathing document, and just like everything else in your life, you can change it. You can change your mind, change your goals, and change your plan.

Just because you type something up or sketch something out doesn't set it in stone. Think of your grocery list. Do you always buy every single item you write on it, or do you sometimes get to the store and change your mind about having tacos on Tuesday and decide to have chili instead?

WHAT DOES A BUSINESS PLAN LOOK LIKE?

Business plans are generally comprised of a bunch of different sections, sort of like chapters in a book. When completed, each section needs to be as comprehensive as possible. Before you share it with an investor or other interested parties, you'll need to make sure it's as polished as can be.

WHO WILL SEE YOUR PLAN?

Speaking of sharing your plan, who will want to see and review it? Well, several people, for starters, if you ever seek money. Whether it's a small personal loan from your Aunt Harriet or a bigger commercial loan from a bank, they have a right to see your business plan. In fact, a bank will likely insist on it. Anybody who's considering investing in your business will want to know what their money will do for you and, especially, how you'll be able to pay it back. This means that they won't be interested in just your numbers but the entire scope of your business.

They may want to know how you intend to sell your products, how well you know your customer base, and if you're a good money manager.

Other folks who may want to check out your plan are landlords (to see if your business is a good match for their space and/or neighborhood or if your projections will pay the rent), potential partners (to see if they like the direction you're going in), and mentors (to see if they are a good match for you). A true-life example of this is when Eric and I looked at potential spaces for our cupcakery. After reviewing our business plan, a local property owner suggested a different location that he had, one that matched our ideas for holding cupcake parties much better than the place we were considering.

Who you share your plan with (other than potential investors) is up to you. Some people tend to get very protective of their plans; I know I can be.

If I was asked to share my plan with someone other than the folks mentioned above, I would only show what I was comfortable with them knowing. For example, if I wanted to share my marketing plan with a PR person or a business coach, I might remove my financials if I didn't think they needed to have that knowledge. Trust your gut.

Rebecca owns one of my most favorite businesses, Queen Bee Creations. This is a company she grew from the corner of a bedroom to a building that now houses her production team and a store. I love success stories, and she has an amazing one.

Your business has grown a lot over the years. How did you know when it was time to expand, either your product line or into a retail space?
I have pretty much just followed the business's cues, for better or worse. The business was showing me that it was time: falling behind on filling orders means hire more production staff. Busting at the seams in our studio space means move to a bigger location. Notice that people are shopping a lot at our really funky warehouse store that doubles as our offices means open a *real* retail store. Realize that people are interested in smaller/bigger/more pockets/different kind of bags and products means develop new designs. I guess it's kind of a listening-and-observing skill, being able to read what is happening and responding accordingly. But the trick is balancing that with also having vision and intent to move toward a goal and not letting the business drive you — or drive you into the ground! I also just trust my gut and my inspiration to guide me to the next idea or product. I find that if there's an idea I am excited about, it's likely that a lot of our customers will be excited about it, too.

What kind of help did you seek out to grow your business? Mentors? Advisers? Consultants?
I have worked with various people over the years. For the past several years, I have worked with the same business counselor — she is wonderful and has helped me navigate so many challenging crossroads with Queen Bee. I also work with my tax

accountant, an attorney, and various friends and associates to get ideas and feedback. One of my favorite things is to get lunch or coffee with other small-business gals and talk shop. I always learn something, and it's a great way to build community and network. After becoming a mama, I've found it especially valuable to talk to mama biz owners.

Are there any downsides to running a business that employs quite a few people?
Well, the bigger we became, the more organized and systems oriented we had to become. This is a good thing, but it did take some of the spontaneity and creativity out of it for me. We recently became a somewhat smaller operation, and while it is a challenging process, I feel reinvigorated to be running a smaller shop. There are more opportunities to try out new things, experiment, and be in touch with the creative process. When you have a lot of employees to support, it's important to be able to consistently sell a lot of goods. Taking on the responsibility of being an employer

is, for me, hands down the hardest part of owning my own business.

What are your favorite upsides?
I get to work with some really funny, smart, talented, skilled, and fun people! I get to provide jobs that involve meaningful work and create an environment where, hopefully, people look forward to coming to work most days.

What's the best business advice you've ever been given?
Focus on what only you can do and what you can do best. For me, that's design and coming up with new ideas. That is my most important job, and I am always striving toward getting more time in that realm. It's difficult as a small business to do that because there is always so much to be done and usually not enough money to pay enough people to do all the work I'd like to unload. It is a constant work in progress. I once read in a small-business how-to book that you shouldn't think that one day you'll have it all figured out and reach a plateau; you will always have problems to solve. But ideally

they will be *new* problems and not the same old ones. That sentiment hit me like a ton of bricks and really helped reset my frame of mind.

If you have investors or applied for a bank loan to bankroll your business, did you have to share your business plan with them? What was that like?
Yes, we have applied for loans, and providing a business plan was a requirement for the process. I didn't have a business plan for the first 10 or so years of business. I basically wrote one so that I could apply for a working-capital line of credit at the bank. It was a good exercise to have to do and we hired our business counselor to help write it, which took a lot of the work off our shoulders.

Have you made any big mistakes in running your business? If so, what did you take away from the experience that helped your business become stronger?
Of course, *so* many mistakes! I wish that I had done more delegating sooner in my business's life. I did my own QuickBooks accounting; we ran our own payroll. I was stubbornly doing things myself (so dang DIY . . . to a fault!) that aren't at all my forte. I'm glad that I learned how QuickBooks works and stretched myself to learn something new. But ultimately I probably should have farmed that out to other people a lot earlier on. I could have focused more on my own strengths and left the number crunching to those who do that best. I am very frugal, and I think that's great to a point. But sometimes the savings realized by doing it myself just aren't worth it. It's important to really value your time and protect the core of your job and vision, and don't let nonessential work detract from that.

BUSINESS PLAN BASICS

We're going to cover most of the components of a traditional business plan. I encourage you to go wild with the areas that are exciting to you, and then revisit the parts that seem harder or less interesting to you. You know that old saying, "Take what you need and leave the rest"? That's what we're going for here. My objective is for you to create a clear pathway for your success. I want you to feel free to dream big and plan hard.

We will cover the main elements of a traditional business plan so that, in the end, you'll be able to pick and choose from the different sections to design a complete plan suitable for any needs you may have. You can even wind up with two different plans if you should choose to do so. One plan, the best and most fun of the two, would be for your eyes only. This plan will help keep you on track, measure your success, and help you to keep your perspective. Of course, you *can* share it with others if you want to, but it may not be suitable for a meeting at a big bank. The second version of the business plan, on the other hand, *would* be more suitable for you to share, especially with the money people.

There are other reasons to share a business plan aside from impressing a loan officer. Knowing how your business is doing is more than knowing how much you have in your PayPal account. You need to know

FROM THE CREATIVE COLLECTIVE: **LISA CONGDON**

I love lists and charts, and when I'm feeling really overwhelmed or off track, I like to sit down and write everything down that I'm feeling worried about. I think it's superimportant to get things out of my head and onto paper. Usually that brain dump turns into a new plan for how to tackle my priorities.

what your big picture is looking like all the time.

Would you take a road trip across the country without a map or GPS system? Or fly to a foreign country and not have some sort of itinerary planned once you get off the plane? Or buy a car without doing thorough research? I'm betting *no* to any of those hypothetical situations.

Don't you owe it to yourself to put the same amount of planning and commitment and energy into your business? Yes, you do. You really, really do.

THE WHYS AND WHEREFORES

Why are you in business? While I'm sure there are lots of reasons, we need to be honest and up front about one thing: money. We all like money, and, let's face it: we all need to earn it. Along with earning it, we need to track it, save it, project it, use it, spend it, sometimes borrow it, and now and then even lend it.

To truly know how to get more money and how to spend it wisely, we need to understand it. Most creative businesspeople aren't wild about doing their numbers, and that's understandable. For a lot of you, your favorite part about money might be counting it. If that sounds like you, I understand, and I can relate.

We're going to tackle money later in the book, but I want you to be aware that everything revolves around it. Every detail in your plan at one point or another somehow revolves around money. Well, money and . . . feelings.

I'm sure you've picked up by now that I'm big into feelings. How we would like to feel determines what we do. I want you to be as sure as you can that you feel good about everything you put into your plan. Doing so will ensure that when you accomplish your goals, they will bring you good feelings and good vibes. You'll actually get to feel your sense of accomplishment and you'll want to feel that way again and again. You'll *want* to do your work, even the hard parts, if you're getting what you want not just financially but also emotionally from your business.

Keep in mind that things can change pretty fast. As I said previously, it's OK if the plan you work on now doesn't work for you a year from now. Business plans evolve and change as *you* evolve and change. It's a good idea to review your plan often and to check in with it. If you're experiencing a low point or lots of highs, your business plan is like your guide.

PERFORMING BUSINESS CHECKUPS

Your business plan is a living, breathing document (albeit in chart or book or electronic-file-of-awesomeness-on-your-computer form), and it's best not to let it stay idle. Mark some dates in your calendar to check in with your plan. Take the time to review and examine your progress. When you look it over, do you still have the same feelings toward it? Is there anything in your plan that you'd like to delete now? Anything you can add more detail to? And how's that mission statement looking? Still in alignment with your overall values and intentions?

Good.

While you've got that calendar out, here is another date that you might consider adding in.

ANNUAL REVIEW

If you worked for another person's company, big or small, chances are you would have an annual review. In your business, even if it's just you and your cat who acts as your mascot, scheduling an annual review for yourself is a good practice.

Choose a date at some point in the future that's far enough away to allow you plenty of time to reach some of your goals, both creative and monetary. If, say, one of your marketing aims is to increase the number of readers you have for your blog or to triple your newsletter subscribers, make sure you actually have enough time to do it. No matter what the goals

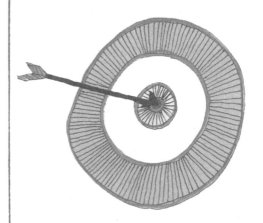

are, you can't make everything happen in a week or even a month. Be fair to yourself when it comes time to evaluate your progress.

At your annual review, take a step back from your role as business owner, with your heart and soul and guts attached to everything you've done. Try to use the eyes of an objective observer. Look at the overall scope of your business and reserve judgment, of yourself and of your success.

What is still working well for your business? Did your ads pay off? Did that line of doodads sell as well as you predicted? Did the ideas you came up with to modernize your overall look work the way you wanted them to?

Your annual review is your chance to do just that: review. Your aim here is to get a good overview of where your business stands. While it's important to notice what isn't working as well as you want, it's equally important to recognize what *is* working as well as you had hoped it would. If you worked for someone else, you'd want them to notice your successes and highlights just as much as, if not more than, your shortcomings, right? Then as your own boss, certainly do the same for yourself.

FROM THE CREATIVE COLLECTIVE: KELLY RAE ROBERTS

I try to check in with myself at least twice a year. I ask myself if I'm fulfilled with my job, if there are goals I want to change or reassess. I rethink my time management, where I see myself heading, where I want to go.

Q&A WITH

ABBY KERR ON BUSINESS THIS 'N' THAT

Abby's career has gone from being a shop owner to being a successful writer and brand voice ally for indie online entrepreneurs who want to make stronger, clearer conversation and enhanced connections in the marketplace. Abby helps people really define what their business is about, so they'll be able to attract exactly the right customer.

Lots of people are afraid to change course in their business. How can someone tell when they are ready to make a change?

You know you're ready to make a change when you sense you've outgrown some aspect of your work, some structure that's integral to it, or some features/characteristics of the audience/client/customer you serve. Outgrowing something can feel really yucky or ugly. You might notice that you hate the way you feel when it's time to work. Or you might not like the way you feel when you're explaining to others what you do, whereas it used to fit exactly right. You might experience heightened frustration in your work or customer relationships. Something feels anywhere from minutely to massively "off," and most likely you're blaming yourself, but it's just a sign of growth.

How can being sure of one's niche help them with their business planning?

The heart of a niche is a well-defined, tightly articulated, ideal-client avatar. [*Note to reader from*

Kari: A client avatar simply means your ideal client. Every single detail you can think about your perfect customer or client makes up their avatar.] All business planning comes back to this avatar; this is whom you're serving. At the same time, your niche and this avatar are *not* one and the same. Your business planning, in which you build out your niche and what you want it to do, is inspired by your understanding of your avatar, the right person to connect it up with. You can't plan an effective business without understanding your niche.

What are some ways people can begin to identify their target customer?
Here's the question to start with every time: Who do I *want* to work with or create for? Not who do you *think* you're qualified to work with or create for, but who do you *want*? Let your response come through clearly and strongly for you. Let it bubble up intuitively. Then flesh out this concept with lots of details. The process is a lot like how authors or screenwriters draw up a bible for their characters. They know everything about them, even if it doesn't play into the story arc or the script in an overt way. They still know. You need to know how your ideal client thinks, feels, responds, desires, lives, opts in, opts out, makes decisions. The most powerful piece in here for you is *you get to make it all up*. You absolutely don't have to base it on a person you actually know.

You owned a retail store for many years. How did you know it was time to move on to something new?
I started *hating* it! All of it. It may sound cold or crass to say that without qualification, but it's true. I realized that I'm attracted to entrepreneurship, branding, and marketing but not specifically to retail. (Interestingly, I love working with retailers who want to understand and conceptualize their business as something more than just a place to buy stuff. I don't work with the ones who *don't* want that.) In short, I started seeing signs that I wanted and needed to close everywhere both internally and externally. It was

right there in my face. The most challenging part was getting OK with the decision to do it.

What are some business considerations people should be aware of if they're thinking about moving from an online store to a retail location?
Location really is everything in brick and mortar; don't settle until you find the hottest one. You'll now need a local, on-the-ground marketing plan. Your overhead will skyrocket with the expenses associated with running a brick-and-mortar store. At the same time, your output for merchandise will grow because you're no longer just showing one of something in a static photo. You've got displays to create and maintain as inventory levels shift. And as a brick-and-mortar retailer, you'll need and want to be in your store — which means no more selling in your pajamas from home!

Chapter 10

DO YOU MANAGE YOUR TIME,

OR DOES YOUR TIME MANAGE YOU?

How you spend your day going about your business for your business makes a big difference in how you'll feel at the end of the day. Spending your time wisely can make or break a business and determine whether or not you get to bed on time.

Easier said than done, though, right? After all, almost no one begins a workday saying, "Today I plan to waste loads of time! I'll avoid everything that matters. I will sit at my workstation and just stare into space, and eight hours later, I'll call it a day." Finding out what your best working style is can take time, but once you find your groove, your days will speed by and you'll find yourself happier and hopefully more profitable.

TIME MANAGEMENT

OK, what does time management have to do with business planning? Do they really go hand in hand? Yes, they do, although they might not look it at first glance. When you're working for yourself, managing your time can be — how should we put it? — a bit of a challenge. Some people can put their head down and just work, work, work. Other people (and I'm one of 'em) can be distracted by dust motes.

For many entrepreneurs, knowing when to punch the clock is just as hard as knowing when to clock out. How do you put in enough time to keep things rolling and still have a real life?

For starters, set some boundaries — with yourself.

PRETEND YOU'RE THE BOSS OF YOU

Oh, wait! Scratch that! You *are* the boss of you! OK. Imagine you're an employee of your business rather than the owner. Would you want your employee spending time watching cat videos on YouTube and updating their Facebook status eight times a day on the company dime?

Let's face it, being the boss has perks. You can start work when you want, you can work as late as you like, and you can wear whatever strikes your fancy. All good news. But with no one above you to keep you on a righteous path, being your own taskmaster can be a bit difficult.

Here are few tried-and-true ideas to help with the dreaded there-is-not-enough-time-in-the-world-to-get-it-all-done-and-still-have-a-life angst that we all go through at one point or another:

Write a job description for yourself. That's right; if you were setting out to hire a manager of Your Company, what would that job description look like? What skills would you want that person to possess? What qualities would you look for? Write a job description that you would find online if you were looking for a full-time job yourself.

Include all the responsibilities that need to be tended to. Write a detailed inventory of the daily activities that you would expect your employee to master. List all the computer or accounting or marketing skills that your perfect employee would need to have. Be as detailed and thorough as possible.

Can everything on your activity list be accomplished in one day? Most likely not. Remember, your employee needs periodic breaks (not counting lunch), time to regenerate, and space to think and be creative and grow. Is there anything in that description that could be simplified? Anything that could be shifted to save time or perhaps even eliminated?

Track your projects timewise. Before you start your next project, big or small, guess how long the task will take you. And then time yourself. No, seriously. Time yourself. Be honest. Include the breaks and the interruptions and, yes, the gazing-out-the-window time (especially if "gazing out the window" is actually surfing the web for anything to occupy your time rather than work on the task at hand).

Start small, and then work your way to bigger projects. For example, writing a blog post. Next time you write a blog post for your business, get out your run-of-the-mill wall clock or watch, and see how long it takes you. What did you notice? Are you surprised at your results? What did you learn? That almost everything took longer than you expected? I know, I know, that is a hard truth; but, just the same, a fact is a fact.

Now move onto bigger projects, like designing business cards for a client or weaving a shawl. Being realistic about how long things take is an important tool. It's good information, and what you learn from this experiment can either set you free or help you regroup. If you find that something you need to do on a regular basis is just taking far too long to be productive or profitable, you'll need to make some adjustments. No big deal, just observe, learn, and adjust.

EXERCISE

Choose a day to test out the Timer Trick (see below). Try three different combinations of time. Begin with 45/15, and then try 50/10, and if you're really feeling ambitious, see how you feel at 60/20. Were you productive and on course? Were the breaks too long or too short or just right? Determine which combination works best for you, and then put it into practice!

THE TIMER TRICK

Are you easily distracted? Me too. I am always on the lookout for ways to maximize my time without giving up the best parts of my day. (Read: Checking social media, reading books, and playing Scrabble with strangers on my phone.)

A favorite trick of mine (and of many Creative Collective members) is properly called the Pomodoro Technique; I just call it the Timer Trick. All you need is a simple kitchen timer or the timer on your phone. Set it for an amount of time that you think you can maintain your focus, like 45 minutes. Then focus on your work for 45 minutes straight. Now take a 15-minute break. Use those 15 minutes wisely. I make myself wait for my break to use the bathroom or get a coffee refill or browse Twitter.

Once you get going with the Timer Trick, your productivity will soar. Experiment to find your optimal time frame. When I'm heavily into writing or researching a client's business, I work best at 50/10 intervals. If the task at hand is huge and I'm struggling, then I try 25/10 intervals. Finally, set a goal of how many chunks of focused work time you want to perform in a day. Six 45-minute sessions amount to 4.5 hours of solid work!

CREATIVE THINKING
TIME MANAGEMENT TIPS

Some members of the Creative Collective weigh in on how they best manage their time.

"I keep a running to-do list, and I estimate the amount of time that each task on it is going to take. I write in that number right next to the task. This helps me to see what is a feasible amount for me to accomplish in a day, and it also helps me prioritize tasks. I also like using a timer for each task; for some reason when there's a timer going, it helps me focus on one thing at a time!"
— **JESSICA SWIFT**

"If it takes less than two minutes, do it *now*."
— **JOLIE GUILLEBEAU**

"Use the particular skills of the people on your team. I was surprised that some of the things I hate to do or aren't good at were some of my employees' best strengths."
— **MEGAN HUNT**

"Don't book yourself wall to wall, from dawn till dusk (and into the night) That's a surefire recipe for burnout, and burnout leads to lack of focus, which means your productivity will dip and drip, and you'll be perpetually scrambling to hit deadlines effectively. Leave buffer space for downtime and playtime. White space is glorious!"
— **ALEXANDRA FRANZEN**

"Walk around the block. It seems like it might be taking up time, but really, it makes you much more productive to clear your mind and be away from the computer and all of those external distractions for just a few minutes. You come back to your task fresh."
— **JESSIE OLESON**

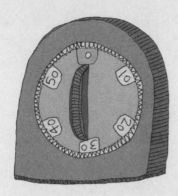

"The Timer Trick! If you need to focus and/or you're dreading something you know needs to get done, sit down and set a timer for 45 minutes. I read that 45 minutes has been scientifically proven as the optimal amount of time to (a) focus on something before you get ants in your pants, (b) actually get stuff done, and (c) trick your brain to sit down and do it because "I can do anything for 45 minutes." Once the timer starts, you're not allowed to look at the clock until it goes off. Just do your work, and know you're off the hook and can step away guilt free when you hear the *ding*. You might even surprise yourself by wanting to keep going, and setting it for *another* 45 minutes!"
— **MICHELLE WARD**

"I do a brain dump every week (or try to) and then work on the most pressing items on my list that are stressing me out."
— **KRISTEN RASK**

"To alleviate organizational overload, try scheduling a specific time each day to switch your activity. You may want to put a reminder in your calendar or set a timer. Also, if your systems are not working for you, then it's time to reevaluate. Ask yourself if there are ways to simplify your systems and make them easier to manage so that they are not draining all of your energy and creativity."
— **KARIE SUTHERLAND**

KEEP YOUR TO-DO LIST IN CHECK

Most people start their days out with a list of things to do. You may even have multiple lists: a list of what you want to get accomplished during the next month, a list for a project you need to complete, and a list of chores you need to do at home. Here's the thing about lists: They can overwhelm you and make you feel bad. Try a new form of list keeping to ensure that you know where you're at and what your true priorities are.

TO-DO LIST EXPERIMENT

Break your list into three different categories. The goals at the top of your list should be your must dos: those things that are the most important to you. You can't stop work until you've completed them. Try not to have too many must dos in one day. Between three and five is a reasonable number. Examples of must dos are connecting with important clients, placing time-sensitive orders, and attending scheduled meetings.

The second category is comprised of things you'd like to get done that support your current and future must dos. Nothing will fall

---

FROM THE CREATIVE COLLECTIVE: MEGAN AUMAN

I tend to work 24/7, and it's only lately that I've realized that if things aren't working for me, it's because I'm burned out. Sometimes, that means committing to a real vacation. Other times, it means not letting myself feel guilty about not working on the weekend. And sometimes, it means getting the bare minimum done on a given day and then doing something else.

apart if you don't get to them, but it would be swell to knock them out if your day permits. These are the things you do when your must dos are done or things you can do in between must dos. Generally, these are things that you can half complete and still have been productive. For example, do research for a project, source a new supplier, or dig out the files you need later in the week.

The third part of your list will encompass the little details that you can accomplish in under 15 minutes. They can come from your intentions and goals, or they can just be particulars that help you stay organized. An example of this for me is every workday I try to file or delete at least 10 emails from my various email accounts. These quick little tasks are helpful in lots of ways. Those 10 emails a day out of my inbox really add up over time! I can also check it off my list, which feels good — plus these little mindless chores are a good way to take a brain break.

FROM THE CREATIVE COLLECTIVE: JENA CORAY

Don't overbook yourself! Be realistic about your time and meager human capabilities (versus the superpower robot or group of clones you might wish you were). There is never going to be more time in a day, so figure out how many focused, workable hours you have in a day and work then!

MANAGING TIME IS EASIER THAN YOU THINK

Managing your time is not as hard as it sometimes seems. Pay attention to yourself and notice when you work most productively. Are you a morning person or a night person? Do you have responsibilities at certain times of the day that you can't avoid, like a car pool or eating dinner with your family every night at six o'clock on the dot? No matter what, you'll have to work your business around things that aren't negotiable. But if you were employed by someone else, in a full-time day job, you would have no trouble working the hours they gave you, right? Your boss would assign you hours, and you'd have to abide by that schedule if you wanted to keep your job. Try to observe the same kind of scheduling principles in your own business.

Knowing when to work and how to work can be key, but so is knowing when to stop working.

When your business is taking off, it's tempting to work nonstop. Recently I had a colleague tell me that she gets excited about a project and finds herself working like mad, all hours of the day and night, for weeks straight. She admitted that she neglects the rest of her life and can only focus on the project at hand. Of course, when she's at a stopping point, she's exhausted, everything else has fallen by the wayside, and she has a lot of catching up to do.

Don't let yourself sink into that kind of trap. I'm sure that at least some part of why you want to own your own business is because you want more control over your life, not less. Letting things spiral out of control because your nose is to a grindstone of your own making is no good. Having enough energy to give your business and your future all it deserves comes from taking care of yourself first. Without a balanced life, you won't be as happy as you deserve to be, and soon all things in your life will suffer, including that business you've worked so hard to create.

MAINTAIN YOUR SUCCESS ZONE

Ironically, staying in your success zone means sometimes ignoring the siren call of your business. It's essential to your mental health, which, needless to say, is essential to your business's health. Consider a few of these tried-and-true solutions:

➤➤ Only check your email a few times a day. (OMG, this one is hard! I struggle and struggle with it personally, but when I manage to do it, it makes a huge difference.)

➤➤ Use an auto responder on your main email account. Let people know when your "office" hours are so that they know when they can expect to hear back from you.

➤➤ Say *no* more than you say *yes*. Claiming some of your time back that you give to doing favors for others will serve you well.

➤➤ Take at least one full day a week off from your business. It's OK to think about your business, but *do no work.* Not one email, not one phone call, and not one task. Take this day and do things you love that rejuvenate you.

➤➤ Exercise. When you need a break in the middle of the day, stretch, walk around the block, or jump on a rebounder, a.k.a. minitrampoline (this is what I do). I also highly recommended one-song solo dance parties. Put on a favorite song, turn up the volume, and dance like crazy for one song. I also keep a hula hoop behind my desk. If I don't feel like dancing but need to expend some energy, that same song I would use for dancing also works when I hoop. Song over, I sit down and get back to business.

EXERCISE

Think of at least 10 things you can do to make your daily life simpler, and then try adding them into your schedule. Can you get up an hour earlier? Can you make your to-do list at the end of your working day instead of in the morning? Preschedule business-related updates on social-media websites? Make your lunch the night before? Write three blog posts at a time, and save two for later? Go on, think of 10 things. I know you can.

Being organized is a skill that can be developed by staying committed to the process and implementing the systems that work best for you. Being organized saves you time and money, alleviates stress, and increases productivity. Karie is a professional organizer, and her specialty is working with creative individuals and businesses, including musicians, artists, and art-focused organizations. Here are some of her solutions.

PAPER-FILING SYSTEMS

Create an organized filing system that works best for your needs and space. Keep active files that you regularly use within arm's reach of your desk or even in a portable desktop file so that papers can quickly and easily be put away. Clearly label files and/or storage binders by project or category and then divide into sub-categories. Your filing system can also be alphabetized by main categories and color coded. Keep extra folders and labels on hand. Purge old files periodically, and shred anything you throw away that contains personal information.

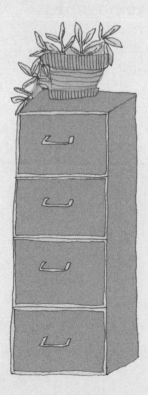

MATERIALS/SUPPLIES

Store like things together, and keep them in labeled/color-coded or clear containers in an assigned and easy-to-use place. Limit the number and length of time that you keep these materials. Take inventory of your materials on a regular basis, and make room for new items by letting go of unused ones.

ELECTRONIC PHOTOS

Safely store your photos online in iPhoto for Mac, Windows Live photo gallery, Flickr, Snapfish, Photobucket, Picasa, Instagram, or Basecamp.

ELECTRONIC FILES

Convert paper files into electronic files to reduce clutter and save time, space, and the environment. Scan documents into a main project or topic file and then break down into subtopic files. If you create shortcuts to active files on your desktop, make sure to delete them when they are no longer being used. Set aside time to declutter your electronic files. Digital filing and organizing solutions can be found online at Shoeboxed, The Neat Company, Blis, Workamajig, Swift To-Do List, Toodledo, Wrike, and stickK.

Chapter 11

THE NUTS AND BOLTS OF
BUSINESS PLANS

Let's get ready to design your business plan and manifest your success! You can create your business plan however you wish. If it works out better for you to draw your plan rather than type out the conventional form, go for it. You may enjoy crafting graphs and tables, or, like me, you may make a killer list that you can rework into something more substantial. I also love to make flowcharts on white boards. Follow your heart, and you can't go wrong.

GETTING STARTED

First things first, you'll want to have all relevant paperwork at hand. Do you have loan documents or a lease or letters from vendors that may figure into your big picture in some way? Make sure you have easy access to your paperwork. This goes along with being organized, which is a big part of running a successful business. We'll talk more about that soon.

Other things you may need are receipts, files, and photos that you use for inspiration or that are a part of your business. Just make sure that any materials you have that relate to your business are accessible and organized.

As we examine all the elements that can be included in a business plan, have your journal handy. Jot down anything that seems inspiring or intriguing to you. Mull things over and come back to anything you feel has promise. You can pick and choose those elements that work best for you. Your plan is for you, and you can plan it, dream it, and design it however you like.

PLAN COVERAGE

A business plan needs a cover page. This can either be a typed sheet with your business name, your contact information, and a brief summary of your business, or you can have a cover page that has a photo or drawing or collage, whatever you like that represents your business. If you have a professional-looking logo or a slogan or a tagline, feel free to pump up your cover page with these images and information. The cover sheet may also include a statement of confidentiality.

EXECUTIVE SUMMARY

Usually the beginning of a formal business plan starts with something called an *executive summary*. Your summary is the who, what, why, when, and where of your company and pretty much sums up your business as a whole. It can contain many different subcategories, but for the most part, you can usually find some mixture of the following:

MISSION STATEMENT

Got it covered! It's hanging above your desk as you read this, right? If you need a refresher, turn back to page 54.

DATES YOU'VE BEEN IN BUSINESS OR A DATED TIME LINE

Time keeps on slippin', slippin', slippin' into the future, according to the wise men from the Steve Miller Band, and they are not wrong, my friend. Keeping track of when you became a legal entity or when you launched a product or signed your lease or opened your online store is a good idea. It's not always good enough to say, "I've been painting awesome pet portraits for the past three years." If you ever need to supply detailed information to your accountant or to your bank for a loan, being really knowledgeable about your time line is key. Just keep track of your big dates somewhere, and keep 'em current. Before you throw away an old calendar or datebook, go through it to mark any dates you may need. Old emails can also come in handy for this.

A LIST OF ALL STAFF POSITIONS

If anyone works for you, even part-time or even for free, keep track of who and what they do. If you ever decide to take on a full-time employee or hire out for services, you'll have a good idea of what you need from future employees.

Even if you hire someone on a contract basis to design your website or counsel you on business matters, detail their services here. If you review this section once a year or so, you'll get a nice big overview of the help you need and the services you pay for. You can use this information to figure out your weak spots and your strengths.

If a friend or a spouse or a neighbor helps you do things for your business — even tiny things that you could do yourself, like washing fabric before you sew it or scouting out locations for a product photo shoot — keep track of it. Why? If people are assisting you, even in small ways, it means you need help, which means these are tasks for your business that you may need to hire for at some point or figure out how to delegate for in the future. Chances are these small things are the same things that cause you to scramble about when you could be doing your actual work.

YOUR BIO

Having a few different versions of your biography is really important. You'll need it for all different kinds of reasons. If you ever write a guest post on a blog or if someone wants to write an article about you or your business, you'll need to provide them with a concise bio. Usually, people will tell you what they want — like three sentences in the third person — but if you're not sure, just ask them what would work best.

Writing your own biography can be really hard — trust me, I know this firsthand. I hired someone to write three different versions for me, and it was money well spent. I struggled for ages over it, but I learned a few guidelines that can make it easier on you. For starters, look through any past press or mentions you've gotten. What is the universal thing people say about you? Begin there. Throw in the name of your business, your primary product or service, and how long you've been doing it. Mention how people can get in contact with you, and then polish it up. You can also mention awards you've won, major publicity you've gotten, and anything else that really makes you and your business stand out.

Your bio should be concise and to the point. It isn't the place to go on and on and on about your-self with every tiny detail of your life and business. While you can men-tion whatever you think is valid, make sure your sentences are succinct.

Be yourself. There is no need to embellish you or your business. You're already superspecial! Don't pump it up or say anything that you hope is true; just stick with the actual facts because they are good enough. If you feel stuck, ask your friends and family questions about your business. Sometimes the impression or opinions of those close to you can clue you into some-thing you didn't realize about your company.

You don't have to use words like "us" and "we" if you run a one-person show. There is nothing wrong with running your own small business, even if it's so darn tiny that it's just you and your dog in the office every day. Working for yourself is a big dream of a lot of people, and you're doing it!

Let your bio do double duty! You can use this information on your About page on your website. Loads of people (including me) admit that this is the first page they visit when they go to a website because we're curious about the people behind the business. On your website, consider having a short version of your bio at the top of the page and a second, longer version further down.

Need some inspiration? Spend some time studying the About pages and biographies of people you like and admire. See if you can pick up any ideas for yourself. I keep a little file on my computer desktop with interesting profiles of business-women I admire and links to my favorite About pages.

HEADSHOT

I know, I know. Not everyone likes having their picture taken. But regardless of how you feel about it, you need at least one. You never know when you'll be asked for it, and it's best to be ready. Besides, people will feel like they have a better sense of who you are and what your business is about if they can match a face to your great products or services.

A headshot is a photo of just you, usually looking directly in the camera.

This is easy to do at home. If you don't have an unobtrusive or neutral background to stand in front of, you can make one pretty easily by simply

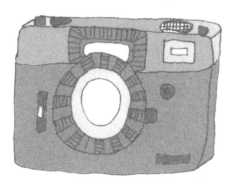

hanging up a sheet or a bedspread or even a length of fabric on a flat wall. (Make sure it's ironed!) If you happen to make something handmade, like earrings or scarves, show it off and wear your product. You don't have to hire a professional photographer to snap your beautiful self. Just ask a friend to come over and take some photos of you.

And when you've gotten your headshot, have your friend snap a few photos of you working. (Customers love to see pictures of people working.) These can be used on your website or any other informational aspects of your business like pamphlets or even in ads.

Once you have photos of you being enterprising and looking like a responsible business owner, save them to your hard drive in different files and sizes. Contacts will ask for different things, and it's best to be prepared for any possibility.

Take note of good photo opportunities when they arise naturally. If you're a party planner, taking photos of an event in progress is always a good idea. If you make wooden toys for children, have some pictures of kids enjoying them. If you have a booth at a craft show or can get a picture of a client passing out a business card you've designed or a painting of yours hanging in someone's living room, these are all wonderful chances for you to get some photos that are useful for your business. And does your workspace or studio look really beautiful every now and then? Take some photos of it when it's at its most photogenic.

If you get a good press opportunity, you want to be prepared. It can be really stressful to need to produce wonderful photos quickly, so keep up with it during the year, adding to your on-call photo gallery.

YOUR CONTACT AND LOCATION INFORMATION

This may seem like a no-brainer, but your business plan should state all of your contact and location information, including:

- Your mailing address
- Your physical address, if different from your mailing address
- The phone number that is associated with your business
- Any email address where you want business contacts to be able to reach you
- All Internet addresses where your business can be found, including your online shop location, your website, your blog, your business Facebook page, and your Twitter handle

LEGAL INFORMATION

Do you have a business license? (I hope so!) Keep that information with your business plan. If you're an LLC or have a DBA, make sure you know when your license was issued, when it expires, how much it cost, and where it is. Do you have a lawyer or work with a legal arts-advocacy group? Summarize your dealings with them, not only so that you have a quick reference but also so you can be prepared to answer any questions about your legal matters if you're ever asked.

JOB DESCRIPTIONS IF APPLICABLE

Do you have a summary of everything you do for your business, from updating your website to designing products or service packages? If so, this is where it goes, and if not, get on it. For various reasons it's important to take note of everything you do. (See Time Management on page 144.)

BUSINESS INVESTORS AND THEIR CONTACT INFORMATION

If you have any investors (and they can be anyone from your Great Uncle Rudy who loaned you five hundred bucks, to your local credit union), their names and vital information goes here. This is where you can keep track of how much they've invested, the terms of the loan, and your payment calendar. Having a biography of each person who invests in your business and a profile of the bank is a good idea, too.

WHO EXACTLY ARE YOU, ANYWAY?

Well, not *you* personally, of course; your business. For reasons differing from your budgeting to your marketing plan, you need to have a complete list of everything your company offers. What is it exactly that you are selling? What is it exactly that you offer? What are your service packages?

Having a complete summary is important. This information doesn't have to be *über-detailed*, just complete.

For example, if you're a knitwear designer, all you need is a breakdown of what you sell. Like:

➼ Accessories for adults: hats, scarves, and mittens, sold in sets or individually

➼ Home goods / gifts: baby blankets, throw blankets, table runners

➼ Patterns: as PDFs only; for slippers, potholders, headbands

Or if you provide services:

➤ Consulting package(s): marketing / branding services offered over Skype or in person

➤ Analysis: complete written reviews of websites, marketing materials

If you're creating a plan for your eyes only, you will not need to include all of these elements, but if you are taking your plan to a bank to seek funding, at the very least you'll want to make a nod in the direction of this list.

BUSINESS PLAN CHECKLISTS

This first plan is for your eyes only. Feel free to add or subtract from these items, retaining the cover page, mission statement, and dates of your business's operation. These are not listed in any particular order. Remember: Have fun, dream big, and know that you can adjust or change your plan at any time. You're the boss!

◯ Creative cover page

◯ Mission statement

◯ Dates of operation

◯ Job descriptions

◯ Tasks / professional work to hire out

◯ Biographies

   ◯ Press

   ◯ Website

   ◯ Third person

   ◯ First person

   ◯ Social media bio

   ◯ Short bio

   ◯ Long bio

◯ Headshots

◯ Product photos

◯ Lifestyle photos

◯ All relevant contact information

◯ Legal information

◯ Industry review

◯ Peer review (competition analysis)

◯ Future opportunities

◯ Marketing plan / ideas

◯ Goals and intentions

If you need to present a formal plan, this next plan is what you should follow and include for your presentation. Other than the first few elements, they are not presented in any particular order. Again, you're the boss, so feel free to add or take away items that you don't want or need. Inquire with the person who has requested your plan whether they have guidelines or are looking for any particulars about your business so you can best prepare to knock their socks off.

- ○ Cover page
- ○ Executive summary
- ○ Mission statement
- ○ Dates of operation
- ○ Job descriptions / staff positions
- ○ Biography
- ○ Headshot
- ○ All contact information
- ○ Legal information
- ○ Investor information
- ○ Industry overview
- ○ Analysis of competition
- ○ Target market information
- ○ Demographics
- ○ Business opportunities
- ○ Recent press
- ○ Marketing plan
- ○ Requested financial information

Chapter 12

KNOW YOUR MARKETPLACE
(OR MARKETING!)

In a formal business plan, people expect a very detailed overview of your industry. The ins and outs, the ups and downs. Why? Well, for starters, they want to know that you are living and breathing this business to the point where you know every single thing there is to know about it. This shows that you are committed to making your own business successful.

Plus, if you are seeking a loan, investors will want to understand everything about your industry so that they can make a sound decision as to whether or not it's something they want to get involved in. Since they may not be that familiar with your creative community or your marketplace, it's your job to educate them from top to bottom.

KNOW YOUR INDUSTRY

What is the exact nature of your industry? What kind of business are you really in? This question may seem simple, and you may be tempted to say, "I'm a singer. I'm in the music business!" or "I am a jewelry designer and I make beautiful jewelry!" and leave it at that. But the rest of the world (especially those thinking of opting in financially) needs to know more. Be as specific as possible with answers to the following:

- What problem does your company solve for your customers?
- What need do you fill for the public?
- Are you a business that serves other businesses (like a graphic designer), or do you serve individuals (like a musician)?
- Why is there a need for what you offer?

Chances are there is a need for the services you provide or else you wouldn't have had your idea to

---

FROM THE CREATIVE COLLECTIVE: HEATHER BAILEY

Relationships with customers are more personal than ever before. Protect your credibility by making sure your brand, products, and customer experience reflect who you are and what you stand for. Remember that you are marketing not only your products but also your business and yourself. Be genuine, stand for good things, and have fun.

begin with. Think back to when you decided to start your company. For example, perhaps you noticed that crafters/handmakers needed help designing collateral materials for their shops, and you knew that you were a whiz at making website banners and designer packaging. Going back to your business roots will give you a nice bird's-eye view of your industry. What initially attracted you to it, and why do you still want to be a part of it?

KNOW YOUR COMPETITION

Knowing who's your competition (or *peers,* as I like to call my competition) is very useful. If you have or want to have a shop or a gallery or an office in your town where you hope the bulk of your business comes from walk-by traffic or referrals, and you plan on doing most of your business face-to-face with your clients, knowing what your customers' other options are is a must.

Ordinarily, you wouldn't want to open up your business right next door to a competitor. Of course, in some cases, this can totally work.

That's why there are places like antiques malls where multiple vendors set up shop, and customers can browse booth after booth after booth, searching for the perfect tchotchke. Or why art galleries are sometimes right next door to each other or at least located in the same neighborhood. So don't be too nervous about it if it seems like a good fit for your target customer. On the other hand . . .

STAYING AHEAD

For the most part, you want to have a leg up on your competition. Maybe you can get a better location or offer more services than your local competitors. What ways can you make your products or services stand above and beyond? Obviously, if you conduct your business online, your competition is a little different. This is where having a niche and being as familiar with customers as humanly possible comes into play.

Keep track of what your competitors are doing by periodically scheduling time to review their businesses. Do they have an exciting new product or service package that they're offering? Are your prices in line with theirs? What trade shows are they attending? You can learn a lot about both your customers and your industry by keeping a respectful eye on other leaders in your field.

I like to make friends with my competition if possible. I believe that my business is good for their business and vice versa. I really like knowing people who are interested in the same things as me, and I love it when they are able to create a successful business and support them in any way that I can. Your competition is not your enemy.

Think about it: Do you buy shoes from only one shoe store or one company? Does your family drive only one kind of make and model of car? Do you eat in only one restaurant? I'm betting your answer to all those questions is *no.* Or at least probably not. That's because you have lots of choices and lots of different tastes

and needs. So do your customers. So while you want to be on par with your competition and keep up on their doings and offerings, focus on being yourself. What can set you apart? What makes you unique?

EXERCISE
It's so, *so* easy to feel like the market is saturated with people who are doing something similar to you. You may look around and see loads of other creative people doing exactly what you're shooting for. When you check out their websites or read their online-shop feedback, it seems like they have it made. You may feel that there's no room for you in the market. I'm here to tell you: THAT'S CRAZY! There is room for everyone, and there always will be. Always.

Get out your journal, and note the online person whose business you covet the most. Say, another painter who gets really good commercial jobs; anyone who you think has it going on for whatever reason. Maybe they're always posting photos of their seemingly perfect children eating perfect home-cooked meals, or maybe their workshop or studio is exactly what you're dreaming of for yourself. Truthfully, they don't even have to be in the exact same business as you. Just pick anyone whose online business / personal life makes your own heart sing.

Now make a list of the following:

➤ What are five things you admire about their business?

➤ What are five things you like about their life in general not related to their business?

➤ How did you learn about them to begin with?

➤ In what ways do you see them interacting with their customers?

➤ What tools do they seem to use the most? Newsletters? A social media site?

Look over your list. Do you notice any patterns? Is that person doing something within their business that you're not doing? Were you able to pick up any tips from what they seem to be doing that you might be able to do within your own business? Think about whether it's their life that you admire or their actual business. With so many people living online these days, it can be easy to get caught up

in feeling bad about your own life or business, especially if it isn't quite living up to your dreams just yet.

It can be tricky sometimes, but it's really important to remember that most people show only the very best of their lives online. They only tweet their funniest lines or post photos that look so dreamy, you can't be sure if they're real or not. Sometimes just to keep it more real, I post pictures on my blog of my sink overflowing with dishes or the mess that is like an art installation of junk that I call a desk.

TARGET MARKET, SAY WHAT?

What exactly is a target market? A target market is a profile of your ideal customer or client. You want to know your target market so darn well that you can predict their next move. You want to know *all* about them, so you can make sure that you are one step ahead of their needs and desire. Plus, you want to know about them so you can market yourself to them and earn their money.

TO KNOW THEM IS TO . . . KNOW THEM

Can you answer these questions about your target market? **Who is your product or service designed for? Who are you trying to sell to?** You might answer: My service or product is designed for parents on the go. My product is ideal for parents who have to travel with their children daily, either by car or public transportation.

Now, while the above answer is good, you can hone the question by asking what I'll call second-tier questions: What age are the kids? Would the product appeal only to parents, or would nannies, grandparents, siblings, or other caregivers buy it? If so, you've just gone from targeting parents to targeting *anyone* who might need to travel with children. Get the idea?

Here's another question: **Why does your customer need your product?** Let's looks at the second-tier questions for this basic query: How will it improve their lives? Will it solve a problem, make a daily chore easier, or just enhance the way they look, feel, or work?

Question number three: **Where does your customer shop or seek out what you have to offer?** Second tier: Is your ideal customer comfortable ordering items from the Internet? Are they most likely to shop from catalogs? Is what you sell best bought in person? Do you sell something that is generally purchased at the same time as something else? Do you depend on word of mouth for referrals and sales?

Next: **What does your ideal customer's life look like in general?** Second tier: How old are they? How does your product fit into their lives? (If you design one-of-a-kind super-elegant clutches best suited for fancy parties and nights on the town, that lifestyle detail is one you want to know about.) Is your target market well off? Or do they have an average income? Between jobs or careers? Are they married or single or young or old? Compile a complete list of everything you can think of about your ideal customer or client.

Finally: **How many different kinds of people can you think of who need what you've got?** Second tier: Is your customer likely to belong to a group or an association? Does your product fit the bill for large groups of people or particular segments of the population? Would it be desirable to baby boomers as well as teenagers?

Get the picture?

DEMOGRAPHICS

Demographics can be defined as a very detailed profile of your customer. This can include anything that could be found in a census report, such as age range; income range; employment status; gender; race; marital status; regional information including urban, suburban, or rural locale (your town or globally); estimated disposable income; number and ages of children . . . the sky's the limit. This information can be presented in a chart or graph form to make the data more readily accessible.

BRAND IDENTITY

Your brand identity is tied into your target market because you need to make sure that your desired customer base knows you exist and gets an accurate picture of what you have to offer. This has to do with the way you present yourself. Is your website attractive to your clients/customers? You need something that fits your style, along with your budget and time frame. Just because you get hungry when you're out running errands doesn't mean you want to go into a swanky four-star restaurant and see what's on the menu.

EXERCISE

Ask yourself: *Does the message I'm putting out attract the kind of customer I need to be successful?* Describe how your brand identity is a good fit for your audience. If you held up a mirror to your target market, is your business reflected? On the surface, what is going to make you attractive to your demographic?

OPPORTUNITIES

Think of some obvious and not-so-obvious opportunities you have to reach your target market. Is there a trade show that would likely bring you extra business and boost your bottom line? Is there another person or business you could partner up with to increase your company's visibility? Do you have some great press contacts that could give you some amazing exposure?

Or maybe there's a new genre of your industry that's becoming trendy. If so, can you be a part of it? For example, is there a fabric or design that's suddenly sweeping the nation? Can you use it for your products? Is there an environmentally friendly option or benefit that a customer would have if they used your services? Can you make your prints with recycled paper or soy-based inks? Can your product be composted or recycled when its usefulness is done? These are all opportunities to reach other markets and to enhance your visibility.

WHAT'S YOUR NICHE?

Discovering your niche can be tricky. Pretty much it boils down to condensing your abilities and offerings to the bottommost line, the thing you do best. What you are most known for. What your customers value about you the most. The thing that makes you stand out. The *something* that makes your business completely unique and irreplaceable.

FROM THE CREATIVE COLLECTIVE: SUE EGGEN

I'll work on a design until it's perfect in my eyes, then I'll photograph it and release it on the Internet. Depending on the response I get, I'll either save the design for a different time or I'll start production. This method has a huge success rate in more ways than one!

Chapter 13

PUTTING IT ALL TOGETHER:

YOUR MARKETING PLAN

Everything you've just done, hard as some of it may have been, will help you reach your clientele. You're now going to be better prepared to find new customers, keep in touch with current customers, and expand your community. Are you ready for the next step, which is also my favorite part? Good! Then let's make a wonderful, profitable, exciting marketing plan together!

TAKING STOCK

As you may have guessed, your marketing plan is the detailed outline, including actionable steps, of your methods for reaching your customers. To develop your marketing plan, you'll want a copy of your goals and intentions nearby because most likely there will be some overlap.

Let's begin by taking stock of marketing tools you may already have in place. Do you have a website, blog, newsletter, and various social media accounts — say, a business page on Facebook and a Twitter account? If so, then you're off to a good start. If not, what's holding you back?! Most of these selling tools are very cost effective if not free, and if you are in business, you need to take full advantage of the services these things can provide. If you need to create any of these things, set aside some time to do so with alacrity.

If you're just now sticking your toe into the social media waters, here's a tip: for ease and consistency's sake, use the same name and avatar. You can always go back and change things up, but we want to get you started. Your business name is best, but if you're targeting people as an individual, instead of as a brand identity, your personal name will work, too. For example, the name of my website is www.karichapin.com, and I can be found on Twitter as @karichapin. However, when I built a page for my first book on Facebook, way back in 2009, I called it The Handmade Marketplace. In hindsight, I wish I had called it something different because although I've built up a nice audience there, it's under the name of my first book. So although I plan on writing lots of books, and I have a successful coaching practice, none of that is obvious from just looking at the name of my Facebook business page.

EXERCISE

Make a list of all of the places where you have an online presence. Schedule time to review each place with an eye for consistent message, themes, and information. Is your business represented well? Is it clear what you do, and are your offerings obvious? How do you use these tools? Are you being realistic about the time they take and the manner in which you use them to communicate with your customers? Do you have any intentions or goals set up based on these marketing opportunities?

Get out your journal or sketchbook and turn to a blank page. Across the top of the page make a column heading for what you are already comfortable working with. It may have headings like these:

» *Twitter*

» *Blog*

» *Facebook*

» *YouTube channel*

» *Newsletter*

Under each category, jot down how many followers or subscribers you have.

Try making a schedule for using these marketing options. Tweak it as time goes along, and find a system that works best for you. Lots of people set aside one morning a

TRACK YOUR PRESENCE

Do you use an RSS feed reader to subscribe to blogs? If so, make sure your own blog feed is being followed. Most services will tell you how many people subscribe to the blog, and this is one way you can get your own subscriber numbers. Another way is to install a tracker onto your website, like Google Analytics, or use a website like www.alexa.com. Look over your personal history with these places, and take note of how often you use each service. Do you seem to blog twice a week? Once a year? Are you tweeting on average ten times a day or twice a week? How about that newsletter? Is the last one you sent so old that it barely contains relevant information, or do you send a newsletter as often as you open your email? How you use these tools will affect what kind of return you get.

week to write blog posts or schedule their Twitter or Facebook updates in advance. If you think this is something that would work for you, test it out and see how you like it.

EXERCISE

Make a master calendar for the year. Make sure it includes all holidays relevant to your customer base. Also include all trade shows, craft shows, or other events where you'd like your business to have a presence. Working back from the dates you have listed, come up with promotional ideas for your online resources. For example, if you sell handmade bouquets (like Creative Collective member Megan Hunt), pump up your marketing efforts

BARTER!

What is bartering, and what's it good for? Bartering is a super way to get goods and services your business needs, provided you find someone who will barter with you. Your best bet is to find someone who offers complementary services to what you provide and then try to strike up a deal. You basically trade goods or services for other goods and services of equal value. Say you need a new logo and business cards, and you know a designer who might need custom illustration work or who wants to give mitten and hat sets to their family for the holiday as gifts. DEAL! Bartering, when done correctly, is a win-win. Just make sure you have the time and ability to trade goods/services and that you have an agreement in place (get it in writing!) of what goods/services both you and your intended are going to provide each other. You can also barter with someone for self-care services if you find someone willing. A friend of mine barters her hand-screened cards with a local massage therapist. She gets a monthly shiatsu, and he gets cards to send to his clients for their birthdays or as thank-you notes when he gets referral clients.

around those holidays and times of the year that are bouquet oriented, like Valentine's Day, Mother's Day, and June for all those weddings.

What are your business's "busy times"? Work those time lines into your calendar and plan ahead to be best prepared. Those busy times are a great opportunity to launch new products, get press, and entice new customers.

Once you have a calendar going, come up with ideas to fill in the blanks. Every time you get a good idea or a brilliant flash of inspiration for a blog post or newsletter content, write it down so that you can refer back to it later. Then take your ideas and figure out where they fit best into your outreach.

MARKETING THROUGH ADVERTISING

Would your business benefit from print advertising? Print ads are actually not a good investment for every business, so knowing how your target market spends their money is a must for placing ads. If your customer base is very specific, placing an ad in a local, regional, or national magazine may work for you. If not, consider other places to get the word out.

These days, there's a blog or website for anything and everything you can think of, and a lot of things you *haven't* thought of! These can be wonderful places to advertise and very cost effective, too.

Facebook also has an advertising program that can put your business in front of people who have an interest in what you make, sell, or do.

Advertising online doesn't always have to cost money. Bartering with a like-minded business-person whose products or services complement yours is a great opportunity. Simply swap online ad space. Make sure you have an agreement in place for how long your ad will be posted and where on their website it will be displayed. Keep on top of it to make sure that it's what you expected.

EXERCISE

In your journal, make a list of at least 10 websites or blogs that your target customer is likely to frequent, and find out their advertising rates and requirements. The sites should also provide you with their reader statistics, which will be helpful in deciding whether that particular place is a good move for you and your budget.

If you do decide to advertise, it's important to track your results so that you can tell if you're getting a return on your investment. Use unique links and your website-tracking program to see if your ads are paying for themselves. Maybe consider using a special discount code to readers of a particular website to help you ascertain the sales that site is generating.

MARKETING THROUGH THE MEDIA

Opportunities to work with the media, both print and online, are wonderful. Seek out press for your business by pitching articles to any publication of interest to your target market.

If your business is in line with what the publication offers to the public, they'll want to hear from you. Remember, they are always looking for things and people to profile so that they can keep their readers' interest. Reach out to them and be available when they get in touch with you.

By the way, working with print media (magazine, newspapers, and trade publications) is one more reason why having a stash of great photos of you and your business is a must. You don't want to get a call to be included in an article at the last minute and have to scramble to come up with the photos they need.

This marketing data can be useful for your business plan, as well. Organize all the information you've gathered and calendars you devised, and put it together in the way that works best for you. Make sure it's easy to read and easy to understand. Remember that whoever reads your plan may not be as familiar with your community as you are, so be clear and explain in detail why these ads or outreach efforts are a good idea.

FROM THE CREATIVE COLLECTIVE: MEGAN HUNT

A few years ago at a women entrepreneurship conference, one of the editors at *Country Living* walked across the room to me and said, "I can't believe you're here! I've wanted to meet you forever!" I was so shocked that anybody who was part of such an influential media source even knew about me. As we talked more, she told me that major media players are always looking for the NEXT story, not the old story, not the same old already-famous people. So I began telling myself that major media sources — editors, writers, reporters — wanted to meet me. They needed to know me. When I met that woman from *Country Living*, my whole mindset changed from "Media doesn't care about me" to "Media has to find out about me! Media will love me!" People are drawn to self-confidence, and you have to expect good things to happen to you while being humble and grateful for the opportunities that come your way.

Jena is the solo woman behind the popular website MissModish and blog at www.modishblog. com. She runs a boutique public relations company that assists creative entrepreneurs in getting the press attention they want and deserve.

How much of a role should a solid PR plan play in forming a business plan?

I think consideration for how you want to get the word out about your business should definitely be thought of at the start of any new venture: Who is this business for? What do those people read? Where do they hang out online? Which editorial outlets best speak to your target market? And how are you going to approach them? Start your research in the planning phase. If you're going to handle PR yourself, make a list of media bloggers and editors you wish to contact once your business is ready for exposure, and get to know their editorials and how your biz might fit in. If you want to hire out PR, research some PR companies in your planning phases to find one that aligns with your brand, budget, and marketing strategies; and factor their cost and implementation ideas into your business plan.

When is it time to hire a PR person?

There can be lots of appropri-ate times to hire a PR person: at the outset of your business to help you get upfront exposure while the newness is hot, for a special event coming up, after three years of seek-ing out editorial for your business yourself and not getting anywhere, or simply when you're finding your [creative] time to be more valuable than the cost of a PR campaign. But regardless of where you're at with your business, it needs to be press ready before you even think about PR. You want to show off your best at its best. Make sure all your duckies are in a row and that you're presenting your business in its best light possible before you start shouting about it from the rooftops. And you'll also want to be ready for what will hopefully be an influx of interest and sales for your business, both technically (with a good shopping cart / back end / customer service team / product supply, or whatever applies) and psychologically (the stress of more orders/clients/work) and even the ensuing windfall if you get a really huge editorial placement.

What should one expect from a relationship with a PR person or firm?

I think no matter what size PR company you're with, whether it's an indie PR girl like me with a boutique agency or a larger firm, you want to feel well taken care of. To me, that means communication between you and your rep should be easy, open, and frequent. They should be checking in with you with questions, leads, new ideas, and links to recent press; and you should be able to check in anytime with them for a little status

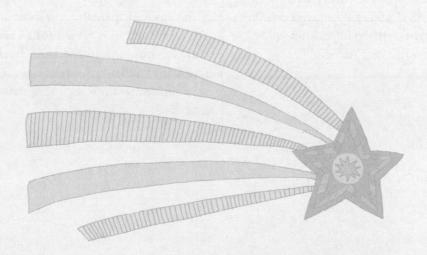

update to see what's shakin'. You'll also want to feel like they have your back, they truly understand your brand and what's so special about it, they will do their darnedest to communicate that message to the world, and they'll stand up for your brand with pride. Make sure the PR rep you choose aligns not only with your budget but also with your brand identity and values. Ask them exactly what methods they use to get the word out. For example, do they send out mass blind press releases to hundreds of contacts at once? Is that how you want your story to be told? Basically, if you feel ignored or misunderstood, the relationship is likely not the right one for you.

What are the benefits to getting help with your PR efforts?

A big sigh of relief, knowing someone else is out there banging down the doors in your name so you don't have to. It's easy for PR folks to sing your praises and brag about how awesome you are! Plus *good* PR reps have established relationships with the press that can aid in getting more exposure, not to mention some great creative marketing ideas for you that you may not have considered before. It can also just be such a time-saver. Researching editorial outlets, writing pitches, organizing giveaways, and setting up interviews are all things that take a lot of time. Having someone to focus on these tasks for you is a good way to allow yourself more time for more makin' and creatin'.

Chapter 14

WHAT DO YOU MAKE, AND HOW DO YOU MAKE IT?

HAVING A PRODUCTION PLAN

If you make a product, you could benefit from a production plan. If you offer services, a production plan will benefit you, too; it will just look different.

READY, SET, PRODUCE!

Let's start with physical goods. This is where it will come in handy to have at the ready your receipts and any paperwork relating to what you make. The basics to know are the following: Where do you source your materials from? What kind of equipment do you use to make your products? How much time does it take you? Create a file for each product and put everything you know about it in the file. Detail the following:

- Name of product
- Variations of product
- Date first sold
- Materials used in creation
- Cost of materials
- Retail cost of product
- Wholesale cost (if applicable)
- Product profit
- Equipment needed
- Time it takes to produce
- Sales copy used to sell it
- Photos of the finished product, including the date they were taken
- Customer base for the product
- Effective advertising options
- How often and how well it sells

When you've compiled all you can about this product, you'll be able to see its own big picture. Ask yourself: Does it have merit or importance to your business? Is it fresh? Is there a demand for it? Does it make you happy to create it, or is it a chore? Do you avoid dealing with this product but keep it around because your customers like it? Can you improve it or change it any way? Those are all pretty big questions, I know.

CHANGE FOR THE BETTER

I'll give you a real-life example of how making changes can mean change for the better. One of my clients knits lovely, unique shawls made from organic wool. Her shawls are amazing, and expensive. The materials and equipment needed are pretty pricey, but these shawls are very high-end. The most basic design takes her at least 14 hours to knit. To make a profit from it and earn a fair wage for her time, she has to market and sell the shawl to a well-heeled customer. Otherwise, she'd be out of business. When she and I analyzed the product, she discovered that it wasn't profitable to keep making them. She just couldn't sell them fast enough to earn enough money to keep her business afloat. She wanted to keep knitting, but she needed a way to make the shawl work for her and her customer base.

So we decided to revamp her line. Now she works on these extra-fancy luxury items whenever she can throughout the year, and come holiday time she hosts an exclusive online trunk show for her customers.

I have one employee who works for me doing production on the jewelry 30 hours a week. This was a pretty easy transition for my business because prior to taking her on as an employee, she did piecework for me during summer and winter breaks. (At the time she was still a student.) This gave me a taste of the freedom I would get from having someone else handle production. Having someone else to take on the bulk of this part of my business has freed me up to focus on other aspects (marketing, sales, Designing an MBA), so it has been more than worth it.

People know that they can get these one-of-a-kind items once a year and that's it; when they're gone, they're gone. The rest of the year, she continues to knit beautiful things but with less-expensive yarns and less complicated patterns. She's able to price these shawls at a much more affordable price, and since she can make them quicker, her profit margin is higher. Furthermore, restructuring her main product has enabled her to send the luxury shawls to an outside contractor for added beaded trim, something she can't do herself and previously couldn't afford to have done.

Do you see a situation like that for yourself in your business?

LICENSING

Speaking of production, a lot of business owners are interested in having their designs manufactured or licensing their work. These are both wonderful opportunities to investigate.

Licensing your designs or ideas means that you enter into an agreement with a company that will reproduce your work on products that they make, like your patterns on wrapping paper or greeting cards.

This is a great way for lots of people to open up another revenue stream of their business. If you look around your own home, I'm sure you'll find lots of products that have been licensed.

Two of the wonderful and amazing members of the Creative Collective have first-hand experience with both licensing and production, and I've asked them to share their wisdom.

Q&A WITH JESSICA SWIFT

Jessica has licensed her designs with many different companies. Her colorful patterns can be found on everything from protective phone covers to thank-you notes.

Let's say I'm a graphic designer, and I'd like to see my work on stationery, wrapping paper, and the like. How do I go about getting a licensing deal?

Many companies have submission information on their websites. That's a great place to start. Submit your work to the companies you'd like to work with, adhering to their guidelines exactly (that's important!), and don't be afraid to contact someone multiple times. I find that I often don't get a response after the first email, but I will after the second or third. And if you can find a direct email address for the art director or creative director of a company, they're good people to contact, as well. Send a short, direct, and friendly email with a few JPEGs embedded in the body of the email. You have to be persistent, and that persistence will often pay off! Trade shows like SURTEX and Printsource are also a great way to get your designs in front of decision makers within companies. Many licensing deals begin with an art director seeing your work in your booth at a trade show. It's important to get as much information as you can from people you meet and talk to at trade shows, and following up with them after the show is crucial.

If I come across a manufacturer of products who seems to be interested in using some of my designs, how can I tell if it's a safe bet?
It's always a good idea to talk to other people who have worked with the same company to see what their experience was like. You can often find other artists' names on the manufacturer's website, or you can simply ask them. Always do as much research as you can about the company before you commit to anything, and make sure you thoroughly read any contracts that they send over to make sure you're not getting locked into something you're uncomfortable with. Have someone else look over the contract and explain it to you if you're not comfortable doing it yourself. Listen to your gut, too: if it's telling you not to work with someone, don't do it!

Is it really worth it to travel to big shows like SURTEX? What are some must haves for my show booth?
There's no other way to meet the people you'll meet at big shows like SURTEX! It's also an opportunity for companies who've never heard of you to experience your work in person and actually meet you and have a personal connection. There's really nothing better! Some must haves for your booth are bold, eye-catching artwork covering your walls (nothing too small because that looks too busy and isn't eye catching from a distance); stuff that people can take away (business cards, postcards, fun freebies, et cetera); a mailing list sign-up sheet (so you can stay in touch with people afterward); examples of your work on products (make a few mock-ups if you have to; it helps people visualize your designs on their product); and, of course, a stunning portfolio.

Say I design fabric. Do you have any tips for getting my own line?
As with paper goods, most fabric companies have submission guidelines on their websites, and they're *constantly* looking for new artists to work with! Submit your work to them regularly and send *new* work each time. They often look for certain types of work at certain times

of year, so you never know when something you send them will fit in exactly with what they're searching for. Submit your work in collections of patterns that work together as a cohesive group, as well. This typically is how fabric lines are produced, so the easier you make it for a fabric manufacturer to use your work as is, the better!

A lot of research goes into this, and it's a good idea to learn all you can about the options before you jump in. Never sign any contract until you make sure you understand every word in it. (This is an excellent time to hire an attorney.) You need to consider the following questions:

» Do I know anyone else who has ever worked with this company? (If so, talk with them about their experiences.)
» Who retains the copyright of my work or my designs?
» How and where are the products made?
» Does this opportunity offer assistance with promotion?
» How much is this going to cost?
» Gut check: How do I truly feel about this?

[*Note from Kari*: Incidentally, if you're planning on either licensing your work or sending out part or all of a design of yours to be manufactured, your outline or proposal for that needs to be in your business plan, especially if you're seeking funding.]

Q&A WITH KELLY RAE ROBERTS

Kelly Rae has built a large part of her multifaceted business through licensing agreements. She has even gone further than just working deals that involve reproducing her art images: Kelly Rae also struck a licensing deal with a furniture and home-goods manufacturer and now has her own line of home items like chairs, mirrors, and other big-ticket items that bear her signature style.

What advice would you give someone who wanted to license their designs?
I'd tell them to go to the Atlanta Trade Show and spend a couple of days

"walking" the show to see if there are manufacturers that they think might be a good fit for their work. I'd also recommend walking the SURTEX show to see if having a booth there would be a good fit.

When you have your products manufactured, you give up some of the control over the final product. How do you deal with that?
I make sure that all of my contracts require that I approve everything before anything goes into production. There have been many times when I say no to items that don't feel right or that don't best represent my work. I've been quite lucky to work with companies that have great in-house designers who do a terrific job manipulating my work for various formats. I'm quite involved in the process, so it's not often that I've given up full control.

In a typical day, how much of your time is devoted to the back end of your business versus the actual creation?
I'd say it's an easy 80 percent. So many people don't realize that the actual creating part of a creative business is quite small, compared to all the other tasks that come with owning your own business. I happen to enjoy both the left- and right-brained parts of what I do!

Have you made any big mistakes in running your business? If so, what did you take away from the experience that helped your business become stronger?
I've said yes to too many people and have gotten myself overcommitted. I've learned (and am still learning) to be more realistic and to only agree to projects that ignite my creative spark. Otherwise, I get grumpy. I've also made some minor legal / contractual mistakes when it comes to licensing with many companies. Getting a licensing agent has helped with that aspect and has certainly broadened my licensing opportunities.

Chapter 15

MONEY, MONEY, MONEY

We all need it, we all want it, and we're all working for it. According to the unofficial poll I conducted with my creative pals (both those who own businesses and those who don't), working on our numbers for any reason is one of folks' least favorite things to do. But, you can't avoid what you need the most. At the end of the day, or the end of the fiscal year, one way or another, your numbers affect every part of your life, both business and personal.

THEY'RE JUST NUMBERS

If you're really freaked out by money, it's worth it to take some time to investigate why. Just thinking that you don't have a head for numbers is not an answer.

I'm sure you love making money, and I'm sure you love spending money...right? So learning to love keeping track of money should be no problem.

It seems like the biggest dilemma people have with money is knowing where to start. How does one begin to figure out this big tangled mess of numbers? Well, you begin where you are. You have everything necessary to get started, and soon you'll have everything under control.

When working with your numbers, it's best to have what you need at hand. Gather up all of your bills and receipts. If you already use accounting software, you'll want to open it up. Or if you're a spreadsheet kind of person, that's fine, too. You can even begin with a simple piece of paper and a pencil.

NUMBERS 'R' US

If you are seeking a loan or looking for investors or even considering taking on a business partner, having your books in tip-top shape is a must. Banks will want to see your budgets for everything: property, equipment, general expenses, payroll, the works. They may even want to see your personal accounts to make sure that you can support yourself without taking money away from your business. Also, the value of your personal assets, such as any property owned or any inheritance you've received, can come into play when you're seeking money to fund your professional endeavors.

This section is going to cover a whole lot of money stuff, so if you're numbers averse, well, you simply need to get over it once and for all. Numbers are your friend, especially when it comes to running a successful business!

WHY KNOWING YOUR NUMBERS IS IMPORTANT

To grow any creative endeavor, whether you want to leave working from your kitchen table behind or you want to expand your offerings, you must know where your business stands financially. And to do that, you must become comfortable with your financial standing. Knowing your expenses, profit and loss, and how much money you're bringing in is essential. It doesn't matter what size business you have now; if you want to maintain it, your numbers will help you do just that.

You can tackle this in lots of different ways. Some people like to do a detailed daily, weekly, or monthly report while others may just like to have a general working knowledge of what's going on and what's going where. Experiment and find out what works best for you. I like to do my books at the end of the month, but I check in with myself in the middle of each month because that's when the majority of my business-generated bills are due. The midmonth checkup makes it easy for me to take a quick stock of how much money has come in and how much is in my accounts.

SEPARATE BUSINESS FROM PERSONAL

Speaking of accounts, it's best to have a separate bank account for your business dealings. It's important for tax reasons that your business money is kept away from your personal money and that you have records of where all of that money goes, including the money you pay yourself (i.e., your salary). It's pretty easy to open a business account at a local bank. If you like the place where you do your personal banking, simply ask them what their requirements are for opening a business account. Some banks may not even offer business accounts. Mine doesn't, so I had to go elsewhere. Most banks will require that you show your proof of business, such as any local or statewide licenses you're required to have, and then you're good to go.

Having a separate business account is helpful in lots of ways.

You'll want to be able to spend money on your enterprise (for things like paying bills, supplies, and various fees) without having to worry about always taking that money from your personal/household account. (Frankly, if you regularly have to take money from your personal account to pay for business expenses, you need to revaluate your business.)

FILE IT!

The thing about having a business is we often avoid doing things until we have to. You might put off separating your money or opening a business account, which in the long run can hurt your business, or at least prevent you from seeing the overall status quo until it's too late. Trust me, you do *not* want to wait until you do your taxes to realize what a financial mess you have on your hands. Save yourself the time and worry, and get your money straight. *I mean right now*! Start today! You can begin from just where you are, no matter where your records are or what shape they're in. Even if all of your receipts are in a shoebox or an apple-picking basket

like mine were until last year, there is still hope for you! Truthfully, your paperwork and whatnot can be anywhere, any place, and you can still get started on sorting your finances out. You don't even have to buy anything to begin getting a handle on where you are financially (which is to say, getting organized). Chances are a quick poke around your home will provide you with sufficient supplies to get going.

Step one: Gather all of your business-related papers together in one place. This includes receipts, invoices, catalogs you use to order supplies from, notes you've taken, leases, licenses, bills, and every piece of paper that has to do with your company. Now get a batch of receptacles you can sort all those papers into: empty file folders, large Ziploc bags (believe it or not, zipper storage bags are steady workers in my personal filing system), old mailing envelopes, whatever you have on hand.

Step two: Begin sorting. Put everything that's related in its own pile/envelope/box/bag. For example, all supplies receipts go together, all invoices go together…you get the idea.

Step three: Go through each pile and sort the contents by month. You can further sort them into other containers or just clip them together. This task can take you a full workday or an evening in front of your TV watching a favorite movie. However you work it out, it really won't take you that long in the grand scheme of things.

The final step: Decide what to do with the sorted paperwork. Your choice. You can enter all the information into a computer program like Excel or QuickBooks, or you can enter it into a handwritten ledger. Again, whatever works best for you is what's best for you.

Ta-da! You now have a filing system! You can update your files daily, weekly, or monthly. I suggest that you keep a basket or another "prefile" receptacle somewhere central, and put any paperwork into it as soon as it comes in. Did you just return from a props scouting trip at your local thrift store? Make a note on your receipt and put in it in the basket to be filed later. Did you just purchase some needed supplies? Ditto.

I knew you'd catch on quick!

RECEIPT I.D.

Always write on your receipts what they're for. If you take a new client to lunch or buy some vintage thread at a yard sale, mark it clearly. Some expenses are less obvious. Say you had drinks with your new web designer. In that kind of case, write a brief description of what your meeting was about on the receipt. If you buy a lot of things secondhand or frequently go to coffee shops to do your work, it can be hard to remember what was what later on in the year. Notating your receipts will help you immensely when it comes to tax time.

COST ANALYSIS

If, like most people, you decide to keep track of your books with a computer, having your paperwork organized into some kind of system will be necessary before you begin using your software of choice. I understand that this can sound like ten kinds of awful and fifty kinds of boring, but you'll be glad you're so organized when it comes time to determine how your business is doing and make big decisions about what you want to do next. Being able to take a quick look at what you spend on what and how much you earn for what you make or do will trickle down to every area of your business.

For example, if you're considering increasing the retail prices of your goods, by looking over your accounts you'll be able to assess if you could lower costs by buying, say, crystal beads in bulk, or even if you're truly making a profit at all. When you're pricing an item or a service, several things need to be taken into consideration.

EXERCISE

Pick a product from your line or a service or package that you either offer now or plan to offer to your clients. Take your journal and list the following:

- ➤➤ The name of the product or service
- ➤➤ Itemized components of the product/service, with their costs
- ➤➤ The amount of time it takes you to make/deliver
- ➤➤ The method by which you sell it and how much it costs you to sell it (for example, if you sell items through an online marketplace like Etsy, note your listing fee, the percentage Etsy will take from your sale, and the cut PayPal will take)

→ The cost of packing materials if shipped

These are your basic costs, which is to say, how much you have to spend just to make or deliver your product.

Here's an example of what your journal entry might look like:

VINTAGE BROOCH NECKLACE

MATERIALS	COST
4 vintage brooches, approximately $5 each	20.00
Clasp	4.00
Wire	0.80
TOTAL MATERIALS	24.80
PACKAGING	**COST**
Box with label	2.00
Tissue paper	0.10
Ribbon	0.10
Business card	0.80
Thank-you note	0.80
Mailing box	free from post office
TOTAL PACKAGING	3.80
ASSEMBLY TIME	**WAGE**
2 hours at $10/hour	20.00
TOTAL COST	48.60

If you want to pay yourself 10 bucks an hour, this necklace is costing you $48.60. You will need to decide if just being paid $20 for your time is sufficient. If it is, super; if not, you can adjust the necklace price based on what your hard costs are.

The point of this exercise is to see every single detail you spend money on to make and sell your products. (If your products use, say, a lot of ink or thread, elements whose costs are hard to break down to an exact amount, simply take your best guess. Or you could keep track of how much you print and what you're printing next time you change your cartridges.) Once you have these numbers plugged in, you will be able to easily review where you could save money if you need to improve your bottom line. Conversely, you could see where you could charge more or what's worth your time to focus on.

If you decide to introduce new packaging or change up how or why you do business, knowing your numbers down to the penny will help you make the best decisions for your business.

NUMBERS NOMENCLATURE

When it comes to business planning and finances, a lot of big fancy words get thrown around, and unless you have a business degree, knowing what they mean doesn't always come naturally. Even if you have a mentor, asking what some of these terms mean can be intimidating. No one wants to be like, "Yeah, I run my own business. Oh, what's that, you ask? What's my projection for this year and my assets? My profit-margin what?" The best thing to do when you don't understand something is to ask. Even if you just ask Google or my good friend Merriam-Webster, find out what you need to know *before* you're called on to know it.

Following are finance-related words that everyone who owns their own business should know:

Asset: Essentially, an asset is something you own that has value. In terms of your creative business, assets are those things that have value that you need to run your business. Your computer? An asset. Your Gocco? Yup. Are you a photographer? Your fancy camera and all those expensive lenses are of course assets. Assets can also be intellectual property. Did you write an e-book? Even though it's not in a physical form, your e-book might one day sell to a publisher, and you'll get good money for it.

Balance sheet: A summary of your current assets and liabilities, essentially giving you a snapshot of how your company is doing financially. It's all there for you to scope out immediately! Your checkbook needs to be in balance, meaning that what you spend can't be more than what you earn. If so, you'll be in trouble quickly. The balance sheet will help you figure that out.

Budget: A plan for your business's money. You expect to make a certain amount of money, and you budget (or plan) your expenses accordingly. If you expect to make $300 at a craft fair, it would make sense that you shouldn't spend $1,000 on costs and supplies.

Capital: Basically, money that you use to invest in your business.

Cash flow: This is the movement of money into or out of your business for a specific period of time.

Cost of goods: Remember the products you sold for $10? The cost of your goods is how much of that $10 is made up of expenses. The lower your cost of goods, the more profit you'll make. Let's say of your $10 item, the cost to you, factoring in the supplies per item, your wage per item, advertising per item, rent per item, and other per-item expenses — is $5. Notice all of that "per item" stuff? To get an accurate picture of what your real cost per item is, add all of your expenses for a month (including your wages!), and divide it by how many items you make over that same month. If you design and build huge steel sculptures and only make one a month, it would make sense that you probably charge a lot for your sculptures. On the other hand, if you can churn out 1,000 baby onesies over that month, your cost per item will be a lot lower, so what you charge will also be lower (especially compared to a steel sculpture).

Equity: An accurate definition of equity would be the value of your business that you own after liabilities are paid. You start a business, and you make enough money to pay your bills and then some. Since you're the owner, your business's equity is made up of the profits, assets, and everything else of value.

Expenses: Things you need to spend your money on to run your business: rent, supplies, Internet, advertising, and the like.

Forecast: Same as a *projection*. These terms can be used interchangeably.

Gross earnings: If you sell something you make for $10, your gross earnings are $10 or, basically, the gross (total) amount you take in. Also called *revenue*. Now go immediately to net income!

Income: Money coming into your business over a period of time. This is the direction you want it to be going.

Income statement: This is a quick page that shows the amount of money that you've brought in over a certain period of time. Income is *good!*

Liabilities: In financial terms, a liability is an obligation. *What?* Yeah, that didn't clear it up at all, did it? OK. Basically, a liability is something you owe to someone else, like a loan. Let's say someone just ordered one hundred of what you make. *Hooray!* And to make this example sweeter, they paid you in advance! *Woo-hoo!* However, at the same time that you're celebrating your newfound riches, you are now sitting on a liability. You now owe that person one hundred of your product, and that order will cost you time, resources, and money to complete. Until that order is filled, you have a liability on the books. Fill the order and *then* celebrate.

Net income: This is your bottom line (also known as *net profit* or *net earnings*). You take your income and subtract all of your expenses. What's left over (assuming it's a positive number) is your net income. Let's look at that $10 item you sold. How much did you make on it? You might be tempted to say you made $10. Sorry, but no. From that $10, subtract all the costs of doing business. What's left over is your net income, which, you'll notice, is a lot smaller than your gross.

Net worth: We're used to hearing this term describe a rich person's status. In business, net worth is figured out by taking a company's assets minus liabilities for a particular year. After all is said and done, this is the amount your business is worth.

P&L statement: A profit and loss statement, also called *P&L* or an *income statement*, shows your business's bottom line over a period of time. Is it making money (profit) or losing money (loss)? P&Ls get into the nitty-gritty and can take a while to enter all your financial data into, but after you do, you'll have a detailed picture as to how your money is being spent, which will allow you to figure out what changes need to be made.

Profit margin: The measure of how profitable your business is. You take your net income divided by your revenue, and multiply it by 100. The percent you're left with is your profit margin. The higher the profit margin, the better, because it means your expenses are minimal and you're making a lot of money compared to what you're spending. If your profit margin is really low, you should take a close look at your expenses because you're spending too much. If the profit margin is a negative number, you are losing money with each sale, and that's *really* not good if you plan to stay in business.

Projection: Also called *forecast*, this is what you expect to achieve for a specific period of time. Usually you come up with projections for money-related stuff, but you can project (or forecast) pretty much anything, such as revenue, costs, number of craft fairs you will enter, or even how many naps you'll take over a month (for example).

Projection versus actual: After the determined period of time for your projection is over, you compare what you projected (or forecasted) versus what you actually did. Did you bring in more money than you thought you would? Or less than you expected? Whether you beat your projection or underperformed, don't open either a celebratory bottle of champagne or a consoling pint of ice cream just yet. When comparing projection versus actual, it's important to go back and figure out why your actual numbers were better or worse than what you projected. Maybe your projection was too dreamy. That can easily happen. Figure out what you did right or wrong, and adjust your new projections accordingly. It's definitely not an exact science, and it takes practice and knowing your business numbers inside and out to be great at projecting. Eventually, though, you'll get an accurate picture of how your business is doing and, more importantly, how it *will* do.

Chapter 16

BUDGETS AND BUDGETING

Money is such a deep and complicated subject. We could talk about it all day long and still not cover every aspect of it. Hopefully by now you have a clearer understanding about why your money is so very important. And because it is so important, let's talk about something we all need, both personally and professionally, but is still a touchy subject: budgeting. Creating a budget can be easy and even fun — it's actually sticking to the budget that can be a challenge.

FIRST OF ALL, WHAT EXACTLY IS A BUDGET?

A budget is simply a guideline for the money you want to spend to make something happen. That something can be a new line of evening handbags or a new service you want to sell to clients or even any old project, like redoing your workspace. To devise a budget, you can either start with how much money you have to invest in the project at hand, or you can make a wish list of what you would ideally like for your project, and then see if that fits in with the monies you have available. Make sense? Good. So let's talk about some specific budgets you'll need to create and possibly include in your business plan.

START-UP BUDGET

Let's face it, starting a business takes money, and when you're spending lots of money, it's very easy to go overboard. That's why having a start-up budget is essential. Before you spend a dime, make a list of what you absolutely *need* for your business and compare that with what money you have. Then, when you begin your buying spree, it will be easier to resist the temptation to buy a lot of extras that you may want but really don't need. On the next page is a basic example of a start-up budget.

First, we enter the amount of money we're starting off with in the upper-right corner. For this example, we had $3,000. Then, as we plan our spending, enter the item, what it's used for, and the cost. The next column is a running total of the amount we're spending, which is a good thing to know. The amount-left column is a simple formula that subtracts the cost of each item from the total amount of money we have, then keeps on subtracting to create a running total of how much we have left.

Before I go further, let me explain why I put the dollar amounts of our expenses in parentheses. Most spreadsheet programs let you highlight a cell (each little box on a spreadsheet is called a *cell*) or a group of cells, right click, format the cell, and tell it what type of number you want. I clicked on Currency

				STARTING CASH: $3,000.00	
DATE	ITEM	DESCRIPTION	COST	RUNNING TOTAL	AMOUNT LEFT
1—Jul	Computer	For business operations	(1,000.00)	(1,000.00)	2,000.00
2—Jul	Desk	Office furnishings	(300.00)	(1,300.00)	1,700.00
2—Jul	Chair	Office furnishings	(100.00)	(1,400.00)	1,600.00
2—Jul	Office supplies	Pens, pencils, etc.	(100.00)	(1,500.00)	1,500.00
2—Jul	Painting supplies	Paints, canvas, brushes	(500.00)	(2,000.00)	1,000.00
3—Jul	Printer	For prints	(300.00)	(2,300.00)	700.00
10—Jul	Frames	For paintings	(400.00)	(2,700.00)	300.00
20—Jul	Tent	For craft show	(200.00)	(2,900.00)	100.00
20—Jul	Folding chair	For craft show	(50.00)	(2,950.00)	50.00
20—Jul	Entrance fee	For craft show	(200.00)	(3,150.00)	(150.00)
20—Jul	Misc. expenses	For show displays	(200.00)	(3,350.00)	(350.00)

with two decimal points (if you don't have any decimal points, it'll probably round up to the nearest dollar, which isn't the best if you're trying to closely keep track of your money), and chose the option with the number in parentheses. In the world of accounting, parentheses mean a negative number. You might also record these negative numbers in red. You've probably heard the expression "in the red." Red numbers also indicate negative amounts. Having those numbers stand out is helpful, so at a quick glance you can identify where your money is going.

As you can see from the above example, we began with $3,000, and by the time we spent our money on supplies, start-up costs, and entrance into a craft fair, we already spent $350 more than we had. This is an excellent reason why you should create a spreadsheet like this *before* you even spend a dollar. You're going to have a pretty good idea of what you need when you're starting out. Just enter what you think the approximate cost for each thing will be so that you can make sure you have enough to cover your expenses. You'll know to try and save wherever you can to make the money last. If it turns out you have extra money, hooray! The bottom line is that by taking a few minutes to enter your potential expenses into a spreadsheet like this, you'll know if you can do it before you even start.

MONTHLY BUDGET

Having a budget will help you restrain your expenses. Like a checkbook, this will help you keep track of your expenses. A budget shows your money (expenses and revenue) over a specific period of time. The following example is for a commercial photographer for the month of July. Each time we have an expense or revenue, we enter it into the spreadsheet. It has columns for the date of the transaction, what the item was, a detailed description, the amount (positive or negative), and a running total of how much money

OUTFITTING

Whether you're outfitting a workspace or looking for common office items like a drafting table or a desk chair or in need of a new lens for your camera, check your local classifieds (either online or in your local newspaper) and community bulletin boards for items that don't absolutely need to be brand new. On the other hand, if you need something that's best to be under warranty or returnable, like a computer or a camera, consider spending more and buying new.

we have left. Let's take a look at the sample spreadsheet below.

For the first of the month, we've had a few expenses like Internet and rent. In the description I made sure to put what type of transaction it is (bill, revenue, expense, and so on), which will help me know where to put it into my P&L statement. The next column shows the amount, and the last column shows the amount remaining

JULY EXPENSES & REVENUE

			STARTING CASH: $1,500.00	
DATE	ITEM	DESCRIPTION	AMOUNT	AMOUNT LEFT
1—Jul	Internet	Bill — Internet provider	(50.00)	1,450.00
1—Jul	Rent	Bill — Studio rent	(400.00)	1,050.00
5—Jul	B. Jones	Revenue — Booked photo shoot	500.00	1,550.00
10—Jul	Electricity	Bill — Electric company	(75.00)	1,475.00
15—Jul	Lens	Expense — New lens	(500.00)	975.00
15—Jul	Lights	Expense — New studio lights	(300.00)	675.00
18—Jul	A. Poulin	Revenue — Booked photo shoot	350.00	1,025.00
20—Jul	Lunch	Expense — Client lunch	(60.00)	965.00
20—Jul	M. Darcy	Revenue — Booked photo shoot	600.00	1,565.00
23—Jul	B. Jones	Refund — Canceled shoot, minus deposit	(250.00)	1,315.00
27—Jul	Props	Expense — Background props	(300.00)	1,015.00
29—Jul	Phone	Bill — Phone	(100.00)	915.00
29—Jul	D. Cleaver	Revenue — Booked photo shoot	300.00	1,215.00
		ENDING CASH		1,215.00

after subtracting it from our running total of on-hand cash.

Looking at the budget, we see the first two lines are expenses for Internet and rent. Then, on July 5, we have some revenue: "B. Jones" booked a photo shoot and prepaid $500. Nice. We then have another bill, for electricity, and then on July 15, we bought some new equipment for the business: a lens and some studio lights. On July 18, more revenue! Then, on July 20, we had a business expense: lunch with a client, who ended up booking a photo shoot and prepaying $600. Unfortunately, three days later we had a setback when "B. Jones" called to cancel her photo shoot. But our cancellation policy states that we keep half the deposit if the client cancels within so many days of the shoot, so we refunded only half of the money she paid us. We ended the month with a few more expenses plus a booking from "D. Cleaver." So…we started the month with $1,500 in the bank and ended with $1,215. Not bad, considering we spent $800 on a lens and lights, things we wouldn't normally buy every month.

You could just log onto your bank's website every day and check your balance there, but with a spreadsheet like this, you can customize it and see a month-at-a-glance transactions for your business.

COMMON BUSINESS EXPENSES TO BUDGET FOR

When you're preparing your spreadsheets and budgets, it can be easy to forget a few items here and there because you use them anyway. I can't stress enough how important it is to keep track of *every penny* that comes into or goes out of your business.

On the following page is a list of common business expenses, such as supplies, services, and fees, to get you started when budgeting. Do you use these things? Are they accounted for somewhere? This is not an all-inclusive list because obviously I don't know your business particulars. So if you don't use any of these specific items or services, leave them out and add in what you need. Think of this list as a model.

COMMON BUSINESS EXPENSES:

- Internet
- Camera
- Phone
- Website
- Computer
- Website designer
- Software
- Hosting fees
- Printer
- Domain name
- Ink
- Scanner
- Fax machine
- Texting plan
- Skype
- Camera supplies
- Electricity
- Lightbox
- Rent
- Accountant

- Bookkeeper
- Lawyer
- Business insurance
- Health insurance
- Local licenses
- State licenses
- Gas
- Application fees
- Business cards
- Payroll
- Postcards
- Payroll taxes
- Taxes
- Flyers
- Other promotional materials
- Production supplies
- Packing supplies
- Stamps and postage
- Classes

- Professional memberships
- Mailing labels
- Travel account
- Pens
- Printing
- Markers
- Office supplies
- Postage meter
- Advertising
- Graphic design services
- Coaching fees
- Craft show fees
- Credit card machine
- Tent

Chapter 17

PROFIT AND LOSS

You may be saying, "There is no way I have time to create, update, and analyze a spreadsheet every month!" I hear you, believe me. So, sure, you can decide not to keep track of your numbers and just wing it. Plenty of people do just that, and they're running successful businesses. The thing is, keeping track of your numbers tells you what's selling well, what's not, where your money is going, and what it's doing. You'll immediately see patterns, which, if you act on them, will make you more successful.

P&L OVERVIEW

The P&L overview gives you the basic "How am I doing?" information at a quick glance.

Mindy is an indie musician who sells CDs, digital tracks and albums, and merchandise, in addition to touring. And this is her financial story. . . .

Let's see how Mindy Musician is doing for the month of April. In Mindy's P&L statement, each "department" (CDs sold, individual songs downloaded, and so on) is shown on the left, with the actual revenue for the month of April in column next to the department. She sold $140 worth of CDs (that is, 14 CDs), $410 in individual songs downloaded, $1,120 in albums downloaded, $2,700 in shows played, and $290 in merchandise sold.

You might be looking at the bottom line of "Interviews given" and be thinking, "Hey, that's not revenue. What's that doing there?" Well, it's your spreadsheet, so you can do whatever you want. In this case, Mindy thought that giving interviews was important enough to include in the same area she looks at to see her total revenue for the month. For her, interviews mean increased exposure, which in turn results in more songs and albums sold. Having this as a prominent focus for her business is good business sense! (Just make sure not to accidently include the numbers from a nonrevenue line item in your equations, or it'll mess up your revenue.)

The budget column shows what Mindy thought she was going to bring in for the month (her budgeted revenue). The variance column subtracts her budgeted revenue from her actual revenue to show how much more (or less) she made compared to what she thought she was going to make for the month. The percent of budget shows how close she was to her budget numbers (more than 100 percent is terrific; less than 100 percent means you need to try harder).

The lower box shows what her business did in April of last year, and

DEPARTMENT	ACTUAL	BUDGET	VARIANCE TO BUDGET	% OF BUDGET
CDs sold ($10 = 1)	140.00	150.00	(10.00)	93%
Individual songs downloaded ($1 = 1)	410.00	300.00	110.00	137%
Albums downloaded ($10 = 1)	1,120.00	1,000.00	120.00	112%
Shows played ($300 = 1)	2,700.00	3,000.00	(300.00)	90%
Merchandise sold ($10 = 1)	290.00	400.00	(110.00)	73%
Interviews given	3	5	(2)	60%
TOTAL REVENUE	4,660.00	4,850.00	(190.00)	96%

APRIL REVENUE, COMPARED TO LAST YEAR

DEPARTMENT	LAST YEAR	THIS YEAR'S VARIANCE
CDs sold ($10 = 1)	90.00	50.00
Individual songs downloaded ($1 = 1)	80.00	330.00
Albums downloaded ($10 = 1)	200.00	920.00
Shows played ($300 = 1)	3,000.00	(300.00)
Merchandise sold ($10 = 1)	90.00	200.00
Interviews given	1	2
TOTAL REVENUE	3,460.00	1,200.00

the variance to this year — that is, if she made more or less this April than she did last April. From the looks of things, Mindy is doing great, bringing in more than she did last year with everything except for how many shows she played, and even then, she was only off by one.

P&L YEAR TO DATE

The portion of the P&L Overview below for Mindy Musician shows how she is doing year to date (YTD) from January through April.

So, year to date, the biggest area where she's falling short of budget, revenue-wise, is the "Shows played" line. It looks like she's done three fewer shows than she budgeted for. At $300 a pop, that puts her $900 down from where she thought she'd be at this point in the year.

She's in the same boat with "Merchandise sold," being $790 short of her budgeted revenue goal for the year. While this appears to be not as bad as being $900 down in "Shows played," it's actually much worse when you consider the numbers. She did three fewer shows but was down almost eighty items in "Merchandise sold." That means people are not buying her merchandise (like T-shirts) either at concerts or online from her website.

MINDY MUSICIAN'S YEAR TO DATE REVENUE (JANUARY–APRIL)

DEPARTMENT	ACTUAL	BUDGET	VARIANCE TO BUDGET	% OF BUDGET
CDs sold ($10 = 1)	680.00	600.00	80.00	113%
Individual songs downloaded ($1 = 1)	1,350.00	1,200.00	150.00	113%
Albums downloaded ($10 = 1)	3,980.00	4,000.00	(20.00)	99%
Shows played ($300 = 1)	11,100.00	12,000.00	(900.00)	93%
Merchandise sold ($10 = 1)	810.00	1,600.00	(790.00)	51%
Interviews given	16	20	(4)	80%
TOTAL REVENUE	17,920.00	19,400.00	(1,480.00)	92%

JANUARY–APRIL REVENUE, COMPARED TO LAST YEAR

DEPARTMENT	THIS YEAR	LAST YEAR	THIS YEAR'S VARIANCE
CDs sold ($10 = 1)	680.00	400.00	280.00
Individual songs downloaded ($1 = 1)	1,350.00	900.00	450.00
Albums downloaded ($10 = 1)	3,980.00	3,000.00	980.00
Shows played ($300 = 1)	11,100.00	9,000.00	2,100.00
Merchandise sold ($10 = 1)	810.00	1,200.00	(390.00)
Interviews given	16	15	1
TOTAL REVENUE	17,920.00	14,500.00	3,420.00

Let's see if there's a trend here and take a look at how Mindy's business activities year to date compare to last year's activities for the same period. Last year, for the same period (January through April), she sold $1,200 in merchandise, compared to only $810 this year. Mindy should go back and see what she's doing differently from last year. Maybe she's no longer offering items that were big sellers. Or maybe the problem is that she hasn't added anything new, and people are bored with her merchandise. Either way, it definitely merits her attention.

DETAILED P&L BY DEPARTMENT

Continuing with the example of Mindy Musician, let's scrutinize the detailed P&L by department. To keep things short and sweet, we're just going to review one department, and, yes, it's specific to the music biz, but the stuff we'll talk about here can be applied to your business, as well. Let's go!

MONTHLY NUMBERS

Starting with CDs, we're going to first look at the actual amount sold in April for each CD. But first, a little background. Each of the CDs represents a very distinct musical style. *I Rule!* was her very first CD, made when she was a rebellious teen, and it's mostly punk metal. Her second CD, *Birthdays Are Best*, was made when she was a lot happier and upbeat and is full of peppy power-pop gems. Her most recent CD, *Time to Drive*, was a more somber, introspective affair, comprised of folky numbers and piano ballads. OK, knowing that, let's look at the numbers. . . .

So Mindy made $140 this month in CD sales. Not bad. By the looks of it, *Birthdays Are Best* is definitely the big seller; on the other hand, *I Rule!* is barely moving.

Using the spreadsheet, let's compare this to what she had thought she was going to sell this month.

Mindy's kind of new to the whole budgeting process, so not knowing what to budget, she just put down that she'd sell a total of twenty CDs, making $200. As she works with her P&L more, she'll be better able to better judge how much she should expect to sell based on what she did in past months and past years. The more data she has, the more accurately she'll be able to determine how she'll do in the future. Her budget numbers aren't bad. Selling twenty actual CDs

CD REVENUE, APRIL	
CDs ($10 = 1)	ACTUAL
Time to Drive	30.00
Birthdays Are Best	100.00
I Rule!	10.00
TOTAL REVENUE	140.00

CDs ($10 = 1)	BUDGET	ACTUAL	VARIANCE TO BUDGET	% OF BUDGET
Time to Drive	40.00	30.00	(10.00)	75%
Birthdays Are Best	80.00	100.00	20.00	125%
I Rule!	80.00	10.00	(70.00)	12.5%
TOTAL REVENUE	200.00	140.00	(60.00)	70%

is a good goal (especially when the bulk of her sales are digital downloads), and she almost made the goal with her new album accounting for one CD (or $10) short of her goal. Her second CD blew past her budgeted goal (earning $20 more than she planned on), but clearly her fans just aren't digging her first CD as she's only sold one, seven shy of what she wanted to sell.

The percent-of-budget column is just a quick way to see how you're doing. If the number is under 100 percent, you didn't make your budgeted monthly sales for that particular item. If it's at 100 percent, you made your budget. If it's better than 100 percent, break out the (in this case, very cheap) champagne because you did much better than you expected to.

Overall, Mindy had a decent month, reaching 70 percent of her targeted revenue. Why didn't she make her budget? That's a great question that could have many answers. Maybe it was just a poor month for sales. Maybe her website was down for part of the month so people weren't able to order from her. Or maybe she set her budget numbers too high.

Setting budget numbers is tricky, but it will get easier as time goes on. She could have set her budget at ten CDs for the month. If so, she would have easily blown away her numbers, but that wouldn't have been very realistic. She knew she could sell more than ten. On the other hand, she would have gotten discouraged if she had set her budget to 100 CDs.

See below for how that would have looked.

Yikes! That's discouraging. While pie-in-the-sky numbers are fun to dream about ("I'm going to sell a *million* CDs this month!"), realistic ones are a whole lot easier to deal with. If you find yourself constantly falling short of your budgeted revenue, don't get discouraged; just lower the budget figures a bit. Again, just starting out, you'll usually be way off, but the more months of real sales data you have for your business, the more accurately you'll be able to predict how much you'll sell.

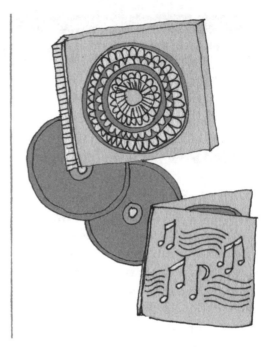

PROJECTED CD REVENUE (100 CDs/MONTH), APRIL

CDs ($10 = 1)	ACTUAL	BUDGET	VARIANCE TO BUDGET	% OF BUDGET
Time to Drive	30.00	1,000.00	(970.00)	3%
Birthdays Are Best	100.00	1,000.00	(900.00)	10%
I Rule!	10.00	1,000.00	(990.00)	1%
TOTAL REVENUE	140.00	3,000.00	(2,860.00)	4.6%

YEAR TO DATE NUMBERS

Let's move on to Mindy's year to date numbers. Year to date (often written as YTD) is the total of all of your sales for the year so far. In the example of Mindy Musician, it's the end of April, so the YTD numbers are made up of the monthly totals from January to April.

For her budgeted revenue, Mindy figured twenty CDs per month ($800 YTD). As far as the actuals go, *Time to Drive* is very "meh" at 62 percent of budget for the year so far. But, hey, look at *Birthdays Are Best*! Judging by the YTD revenue, it's really been a hot-selling CD for her, coming in at 200 percent of her budgeted revenue. However, *I Rule!* does not at all rule, sitting at just 16 percent of budget.

Year to date, Mindy made $790 on CD sales. Her total budgeted revenue was $800, meaning she was just $10, or just one CD, shy of budget overall. That's nice.

If I were Mindy, I would think back and figure out why *Birthdays Are Best* was such a huge seller. "Hey, wait a second!" you may be saying. "Why not try and figure out why the other two aren't selling well?" Yes, you can do that, but I find it's easier and more productive to focus

CD REVENUE YEAR TO DATE (JANUARY TO APRIL)

CDs ($10 = 1)	ACTUAL	BUDGET	VARIANCE TO BUDGET	% OF BUDGET
Time to Drive	100.00	160.00	(60.00)	62%
Birthdays Are Best	640.00	320.00	320.00	200%
I Rule!	50.00	320.00	(270.00)	16%
TOTAL REVENUE	790.00	800.00	(30.00)	98%

on the positive aspects of things. Sure, you can try to figure out why the other two albums aren't doing great. Maybe it's the offensive cover art. Maybe it's the 20-minute songs made up of nothing but baseball bats hitting concrete. Maybe Mindy's put more into promoting *Birthdays* than her other two CDs. Maybe they could be better sellers with more attention . . . or maybe people just like *Birthdays* better. With limited time, I would focus on what's selling well and keep doing it.

What made *Birthdays Are Best* the big seller it is? Most likely people are enjoying the peppier music. When focusing on that album, Mindy should look at her marketing efforts. Maybe she made a video from that CD that's really popular, or she did an interview with a big newspaper, blog, or magazine. Maybe a very popular musician tweeted that they were listening to it. However you look at it, Mindy has learned a lot from this spreadsheet so far. What she decides to do with that knowledge is up to her. Creatively, she needs to consider which albums are selling well and why, and perhaps use that information to plot her musical direction while still allowing herself to grow as an artist. Mindy might want to strive for a good balance between *I Rule!* and *Birthdays Are Best*, doing what she wants creatively while keeping it close enough to her successful album to maximize her creativity and her sales.

The same goes for any type of creative business, including yours. Do you sell photographs? Knitting patterns? Jewelry? Short stories? After you do a detailed P&L like this, you'll likely discover that some of your items probably hardly sell, but others are huge sellers.

While you may have a general idea of how well things sell, this will give you exact numbers that you can use to make informed decisions to chart the course of your business. Drop the dead weight and analyze why your best sellers are so popular.

Chapter 18

MONEY AND HOW TO GET SOME

Now that we've covered money that you *do* have, let's talk about money you *don't* have but want. If you are considering getting a loan for your business, you have some options. Banks, grants, family members, angel investors, and community resources are all legitimate paths. As you decide who you want to approach, take note of what their requirements are for requesting money. Different institutions and different people may want different information from you.

BANK LOANS

Let's start with banks since they're the most common way to get money for any business. Banks are actually pretty easy to work with. I don't mean it's always easy to get money from them, but dealing with them is very straightforward. First of all, banks want to lend you money, and they are very clear about what you need to do to apply for a loan.

Make an appointment to speak with the loan officer at the bank where you have your business account. Show up prepared, knowing exactly what you want the bank to do for you. Do you want a loan for equipment like new ovens or industrial sewing machines, or do you need money to renovate your working space? Do you need a line of credit to buy whatever your business might require over the next two years? Be really clear about what you want the money for and why. Be prepared to talk about your business and to answer any questions that you think may come up. Make sure that you can expertly explain just what it is you do.

Bring a list of questions regarding applying for the loan, including how long the process can take because the time it takes for approval can vary greatly from bank to bank. You should walk out of this meeting knowing anything and everything that the bank will want from you

WHICH BANK SHOULD YOU BANK ON?

Not sure which bank you should open an account at or apply for a loan with if you don't already have a business banking relationship established? Contact your nearest Small Business Administration office and ask them which local lenders are friendly toward small-business owners. Most SBAs are on excellent terms with at least a few banks and lenders, and they will gladly point you in the right direction.

when it comes time for them to make a decision about lending you money. In fact, ask for a loan application so that you can see what questions you'll need to answer. And ask the loan officer if the bank has any local resources or organizations that they work with when it comes to lending money to small businesses. Once you have all this information, get to work applying for the loan.

GRANTS

In the United States, grants are available for any number of purposes. You can search for local, state, or national grants at your local library or online. To apply for a grant, find one that matches your needs and simply submit an application. Grant applications come with guidelines and are usually pretty straightforward about what is expected from you. If you are awarded a grant, it usually comes with stipulations like how long you have to complete the project and maybe even parameters about what you can do with the money once you receive it. Make sure you can comply with these guidelines before accepting (or even applying for) the money. Grants are highly competitive, and if you win one, it means others have lost out, so be sure that it's a good match for you. Plus, applying for a grant takes a lot of effort, and if you don't truly agree with the stipulations of the grant, don't waste your time going through the application process.

Grants are an especially excellent source of funding for artists of all stripes, from painters to printmakers to photographers to writers.

FROM THE CREATIVE COLLECTIVE: ALISON LEE

Don't doubt your intuition, and be real about your overhead. You can juggle numbers, but they never lie.

GRANT WRITING

Writing a grant can be daunting, but you can get help. Lots of professional grant writers are employed by nonprofits, and most of them work as freelancers on the side. Check Craigslist and see if anyone near you is offering their services. If not, post an ad seeking help. Most freelance grant writers take a cut of the grant money awarded, and you can work out a fee that suits you both. You can also suggest bartering for their services if you create something the grant writer might be interested in. A painting or handmade goods in exchange for a professional writer's skills might satisfy both parties! In any regard, getting professional help with winning a grant is an excellent investment.

If you make large-scale works, like bronze sculptures or murals, applying for a grant is a great way to have money for your project and get exposure, as well.

ANGEL INVESTORS

Angel investors are groups of people (or in some cases, one person) who pool their money to support business ideas. Most angel-investor groups work with large sums of money, but smaller investment groups are becoming more popular, and many of these like to keep their investment dollars local.

These groups (or individuals) work in lots of different ways, so be sure you know that the angel(s) you're approaching fits well with your business and you personally. Sometimes you pay the loan back, and sometimes the investors take part ownership control and get paid back through your profits.

HOW DID YOU GET THE MONEY TO START YOUR BUSINESS?

Securing financing for your business is a pretty important detail. After all, most businesses need at least some money to begin with, even if it's just to upgrade your computer or buy that first hunk of clay to throw on your wheel. There are as many ways to get funds as there are things you need funds for. Your naturally creative thinking skills can really help you with this, so don't leave any stone unturned or any viable possibility overlooked. Here's how some of the Creative Collective members financed their business dreams.

"I started my business when I was 23, after my very first juried art show. It was a major success and an eye-opening experience that led me to realize that I could make a living as an artist. I've always been good at saving money, so I used what savings I had to live off of while I was preparing for that first show (I'd quit my job as a waitress to focus on painting), and then it all started snowballing after that. I entered more shows and was very successful in the beginning, so it sort of funded itself. Plus, I was 23 and didn't have tons of expenses yet!"
— JESSICA SWIFT

"I have always been good at saving, and when I started my business, I realized that this was the 'rainy day' I'd been saving for all along, that this business was a worthy cause to dip into the savings."
— JESSIE OLESON

"I don't believe in carrying debt, and thankfully my business required very little to get started. Just sup-plies and a blogspot. As things

223

sold, I paid for a professional site design and bought a fancy printer, but there was very little overhead in the beginning. Now I have my own studio and equipment, but I began by bartering, borrowing, or getting creative with what I already had."
— **JOLIE GUILLEBEAU**

"I worked full-time and then part-time until I got to the point where I was making enough at my art and illustration work to become a full-time artist."
— **LISA CONGDON**

"I applied for all of the college scholarships I could, went to the school that gave me the most money, graduated without debt, and saved every penny to reinvest in my business. Growing slowly enabled me to manage the cost of overhead, and I didn't hire employees until they were necessary to continue on my growth trajectory. I think I have an irrational fear of business loans and investors. I just hate owing money."
— **MEGAN HUNT**

"Since my business is service oriented, I didn't have any traditional start-up costs in terms of renting a workspace or buying materials and so on. Frankly, I simply scrabbled and saved for about six months at my 9-to-5 gig to ensure that I could comfortably coast for a spell if the clients didn't come a-knockin' right away. Just before starting my entrepreneurial adventure, I invested in a twelve-session package with a stellar career coach named Michelle Ward. I wanted professional guidance, hand-holding, accountability, and heartfelt support — quitting your *j-o-b* in the midst of the Great Recession ain't no cakewalk, after all! Michelle was a rock star, and I'm forever indebted to her brilliance. I also invested about $2,500 in a professionally designed website and blog, which elevated my online presence (and client attraction) dramatically."
— **ALEXANDRA FRANZEN**

"For my current business — a digital, work-from-anywhere one — I earned the minimal start-up costs by doing client work that I carried

over from consulting less 'officially' while I was closing my first business (a brick-and-mortar retail shop). I feel wildly blessed and tremendously smart that my current business can be run quite low cost."
— **ABBY KERR**

"I funded my business from the tiny — and I mean *tiny* — bit of extra from my husband's paycheck for the first couple months of my business. I also put some minor expenses on a personal credit card. I took a lifestyle loan from our credit union to bankroll the purchase of an existing business. The monthly payments and interest were clearly going to be more than covered by the extra revenue this business would generate for me."
— **TARA GENTILE**

"Giant Dwarf started from a sweater folded neatly in my closet. I decided to reconstruct it into my first Fleurette Cloche and sold it right off my head. Beyond that, I only spent what I had from my other job at the time on supplies until I was able to create a nest egg from sold items.

I knew I didn't want to get a small-business loan, so I had to be really smart about how I spent my money."
— **SUE EGGEN**

"For the first year or two of running my business, I was pretty much bootstrapping. I'd go to a show, sell things, and then invest that money back into running the business. But in late 2008, I made the decision to attend a big trade show and didn't have the funds to afford it on my own, so I took out a line of credit at a local bank. I combined that with a business credit card to really help fund my business when things were slow in 2009. Now, I'm back to making sure my business is self-funding."
— **MEGAN AUMAN**

"I worked a full-time job and slowly built my business in the evenings and on weekends. Over time, my full-time job became a part-time job, and then I was able to quit once I was able to consistently make enough monthly income from my business."
— **KELLY RAE ROBERTS**

CROWD-FUNDING

Not so very long before I decided to write this book, a new trend in raising money for businesses and creative ideas came onto the scene: crowd-funding. Anyone can utilize such websites as Kickstarter or Indiegogo (where you ask for money for your business and don't pay it back). So the possibility of securing some money for your big idea has never been easier.

I am a huge fan of crowd-funding, and if I was looking for money to fund a project or equipment to make my business run smoother or a way to raise money to record a CD or pay for the one class that could change everything, it would be something I would try. The premise of crowd-funding is you simply ask the good people of the world to fund your dream. You tell them what you want to do and why it's not only important to you but also the effect it will have on your community and the world at large — and then you ask them to support it with their dollars.

JESSICA SWIFT ON CROWD-FUNDING

In the spring of 2011, I decided to create a Kickstarter project to raise funds for a line of patterned rain boots with secret messages on the inside that I wanted to make. I'd spent several months earlier in the year working with a manufacturing partner to source a factory that could produce the boots for me, figuring out all the cost details and creating the patterns and the concept for the boots. But there was one catch: I didn't have the $18,000 in my business bank account needed to place an order with the factory and get the line of boots off the ground.

That's when I decided to give Kickstarter a go. I thought it would not only be the perfect way to raise the funds but also to spread the word about what I was up to, get people excited, and have one of the Kickstarter backer rewards be a pair of the boots! [*Note:* The rewards are an essential part of using Kickstarter — people who pledge money to your project get a reward in return that's directly related to the project, and the more they donate, the better the reward!] So once the boots were produced and I'd sent them out as rewards, hundreds of pairs of boots would already be walking around the streets before I even started selling them. It seemed like the perfect solution!

It was pretty simple to start the project. I sent in my proposal, it was accepted the same day, and then I got to work. A friend helped me create my promo video that explained what the project was about, I created a whole bunch of mocked-up boots with my patterns on them to show people what they would look like, I made button graphics for people to use on their own websites and blogs to help me spread the word about the project, I decided what my backer rewards would be — and then I was ready to go!

Pushing the Publish Project button was scary and exhilarating. So many thoughts swirled around my head: *What if I don't raise the money? What if people think it's a stupid idea? What if someone copies me and gets the boots out before I do?* But I pushed through those fears and launched the project anyway — and thank goodness I did because the project ended up getting fully funded after just two weeks! It was truly incredible.

I spread the word (and urged other people to help me) through Twitter and Facebook as well as on my own blog and website, and I give social media tons of credit for the success of the project. People really latched onto the idea and helped me make it a reality. I'll be forever grateful to everyone who helped me spread the word far and wide!

FAMILY AND FRIENDS

Sometimes borrowing money from family and friends may seem like your best and possibly only option. However, with that in mind, I caution you against doing it if you have any other choices.

First of all, owning a creative business is an incredibly personal thing. Creativity and artistic expression don't follow any kind of rules or formulas. Creative people are generally in business for themselves because they have a calling. Something wonderful inside compels them to create, to share their ideas and their visions with the world. These amazing folks are not all about the money and are usually not looking for a way to earn money that simply boosts their bank account — although of course that is welcomed! When you're putting your heart and soul and your own dollars plus all your hopes and dreams into your business, and your very happiness hangs in the balance of it being successful or not...well, sometimes it's best to leave people who are close to you out of the equation if possible.

These are not anonymous funding sources; they are the people who care and love you the most in the world. Their only desire is for your success and happiness, and if you take money from them, you have to be willing to invite their advice and criticism along with their checks.

And if you change business directions or don't use that pricey piece of equipment you borrowed money for as much as you originally thought, you may have some explaining to do at the family reunion. However, a banker will never know if that vintage letterpress has gotten a wee bit dusty.

If, after taking your personal-relationship dynamics into consideration, you still think that approaching someone you know and love for a loan is the very best idea, do it in the smartest and most professional way you can. If you begin this new phase of your relationship in a serious and businesslike manner, you may be able to set the tone for this aspect of your relationship.

Present your chosen lender with a business plan that will assure them that:

➨ You're an expert

➨ You're a professional businessperson

➨ You're a good and trustworthy candidate for their money

➨ You take your business very, very seriously

Be extremely direct and clear with your request and your expectations. Take this money-lending relationship very conscientiously and be open minded when it comes to payment terms and interest rates. Listen carefully to what your investment partner wants and thinks. Answer all their questions and make sure you ask any questions of your own. Go above and beyond to instill utmost trust in you and your ability to use their money wisely, and treat their investment with the utmost respect.

If someone you know personally lends you money to further your business, it's not just because you have awesome skills and fantastic ideas; it's mostly because they believe in you, they believe in your dreams, and they want you to be happy and successful. Plus they think you have awesome skills and fantastic ideas. . . .

LARGE LARGESSE

When taking a sizable loan from someone you know, it's best to get a lawyer involved. A lawyer can help you draft documents that clearly outline the lender's expectations as well as your responsibilities. This is an extra expense, sure, but you want to protect yourself and your business 100 percent. Plus, it might just impress the person lending you the money by how serious you are! If you don't want the law on your side, do your very best to draft documents yourself that clearly define your responsibilities and your repayment plan. Get everything in writing. When it comes to money, especially major amounts of money, handshake deals just won't do.

FINANCING WITH PERSONAL CREDIT CARDS

We've all done it, and most likely we're all gonna do it again at some point: you're going to whip out a credit card to pay for a business expense. Maybe it's for an emergency purchase, or maybe you forgot about an alternative payment method, but quite possibly it'll be because it's your only option.

Using credit cards to pay for monthly or weekly expenses can be risky, and if you can avoid it, please do. Just as your personal credit card debt can quickly add up, the same goes for your business spending — and if you've spent your credit on your business, it may not be there when you need it for personal expenses.

Sure, there are lots of wonderful stories out there in the world about people who've accomplished amazing things by only using credit cards as their funding source. So it's not that it can't be done. It's just that it's risky.

If you do need to rely on plastic to make purchases, here are a few things you should be aware of:

Know what your charge cards are really costing you. What are the terms of your card, and what are the interest rates? If you can, try to negotiate a lower rate with your credit card company. If you've had your card for some time and you've always paid your bill on time, or if you pay a bit extra toward your

FROM THE CREATIVE COLLECTIVE: **MEGAN AUMAN**

About the only thing I truly wish I had done differently was committing earlier to putting money into savings. Having a cushion of savings really has made a big difference in my stress level, as I now feel more able to ride the ups and downs of my business.

balance each month, simply call them up and let them know that you'd like a lower rate. If they can, they may lower it for you. It's a good idea to know what your lowest rate is on your cards because sometimes lenders will ask you what sort of rates they're competing with, and you'll want to be able to answer knowledgeably.

Know if you're rewarded for paying balances off by a certain date. Do you earn points toward something useful like air miles that could help get you across the country for craft fairs or trade shows? If so, use that card to your business's advantage.

If at all possible, don't use your cards to get cash. The interest rate and penalties for missing a payment can be even higher for those tempting cash advances. If you have to do it, know what that rate is and then calculate how much it is going to cost you in cold hard cash to pay back that cash advance. You may be surprised and then motivated to find a better way to get what you need.

Know if your credit card carries warranty options. If you can score extended warranties on big-ticket items like a computer through your credit card company, then using one may be in your business's best interest, but make sure you understand the conditions before you buy.

I was encouraged early on to put inventory and other expenses on my credit cards. BIG mistake. When a bill came and I didn't have the funds to pay off the balance in full, I started accumulating debt that became difficult to pay off. I now use a debit card for nearly everything. It can be painful at times, but it keeps me honest about my finances.

FINDING A WAY

No matter the state of your financial affairs, you can do this. Lots of businesses that started with nothing, or next to nothing, are now great successes. There is nothing out there that says the same can't or won't happen for your business. If you're feeling low because of dollars, or a lack thereof, try to spend some time focusing on the parts of your business that don't require your wallet at the moment. Look at your marketing plan again, organize your supplies, or try out some new social media strategies.

Remember, some of your most valuable skills have nothing to do with your bottom line. Your creativity and ability to dream and shape your future aren't a reflection of what's in your business bank account. Take those skills and use them to the fullest. Give yourself enough space and time to get your work done. Take care of yourself. Give yourself breaks, both emotional and physical, when you need them. And if you hit a rough patch, reach out to your community. Celebrate your successes and be proud of what you're accomplishing. Keep in mind how amazing you are.

Focus on how you want your business to make you feel, and then let the rest take care of itself. You've got things that money cannot buy and lack of money cannot stifle.

Chapter 19

MAKING IT ALL LEGIT

When you're in business for yourself, you must attend to all aspects of your endeavor, and the legal side of things can't be ignored. How you've set up your enterprise in the eyes of the law is very, very important. If you have a retail shop, you must have insurance. If you make edibles or cosmetics, insurance is a good idea, too. In fact, insurance for your business is an important consideration no matter what you do.

If you need to sign a lease, you might want to consider having a lawyer look things over. Ditto if you do something that requires signing a contract and you don't have an experienced agent by your side. Legal stuff doesn't *always* involve lawyers. However, almost all legal stuff costs some amount of money one way or another. Bummer.

WHAT KIND OF BUSINESS ARE YOU?

Essentially, small businesses fall into three main types: sole proprietorship, partnership, and limited liability company (LLC), but all three have subcategories. This means that there are actually lots of choices when it comes to declaring what type of business you are. All have many ins and outs, so taking a good look at what you do and what you want will require some work on your part. This is a pretty important step, and while you can always change your mind, think long and hard about what form of business will be best for you.

No matter what you choose, if you plan on selling something under any name other than your own, call your local county clerk and learn how to register your DBA (doing business as) name. This prevents you from using someone else's name or someone else using your name.

Incidentally, your legal declaration needs to be in your business plan. And any paperwork that revolves around it needs to be filed. And by the way, if you have to renew your business license annually, don't forget to include that fee in your budget!

Let's examine the three main types of businesses that you can declare:

SOLE PROPRIETOR

A sole proprietor is an unincorporated business. If you run your business with no employees, do freelance or contract design, or do craft work, you may be a sole proprietor. This is the easiest kind of business to start. You pretty much just have to declare yourself a sole proprietor and then claim what you earn when you do your taxes the following year. You'll need to fill out a special tax form called a Form 1040 Schedule C. As a sole proprietor, you are 100 percent responsible for what you do. This means if legal issues arise, like someone gets sick or injured from something you sold them, you alone must take responsibility. It would be possible for someone to sue you personally if they wanted to. Also, if you take out a loan to help your business, you are personally responsible for repaying the debt.

PARTNERSHIP

So you and your BFF want to go into business together. In that case, you may want to consider forming a partnership. This takes more legwork or paperwork than a sole-proprietor setup, but all those extras will help you down the line if one of you wants to buy out the other one or leave the business for any reason. As in any relationship, boundaries need to be acknowledged, and in this case all the assets you and your partner bring to the cutting table need to be spelled out. This means deciding

KNOW YOUR LOCAL LEGALITIES

People from all over the world read and need these kinds of business books. This is, of course, good for writers like me. But I must state here that I am an American, and therefore I best know what happens in the United States. The laws and rules you must follow where you live may be different from what I am qualified to discuss here, and I urge you to become familiar with the rules, regulations, and policies in your country. And for all of you fellow U.S. citizens, legal rules can vary from state to state and even town to town! It is your responsibility to be aware of what the law requires of you in your specific locale.

who is responsible for what, as in money coming in and money going out of the business; delineating roles and duties; and other business-related minutiae. Hashing out and defining these details is important because as with a sole proprietorship, the law does not separate you personally from your business under a partnership, so all partners can be held legally responsible if something goes wrong.

LIMITED LIABILITY COMPANY (LLC)

An LLC can be owned by one person or a group of people. The primary benefit of an LLC is that you are separated personally from your business, meaning if something were to go wrong, only your business could be sued, not you personally. While you aren't completely free from liability with this option (hence the name *limited* liability), you are only responsible for what you put

ENTERING INTO PARTNERSHIPS

We've all seen it happen in our creative community. We meet a like-minded soul online or at a show and immediately want to partner up on a project. Maybe you want to create an online course with someone, or coauthor a downloadable book. Perhaps you saw their paintings and were hit with the inspiration to create a line of paper goods with them. If you should find yourself in a situation like this, good for you! I believe in partnerships and love nothing more than a good old-fashioned creative collaboration.

For the benefit of both you and your partner, though, you need to make sure you're legally protected. Even with the best of intentions, pinky swears, and being best blog friends forever, things can sometimes . . . go awry. Start off on the right foot and make it legal when you seal the deal.

into it financially. When it comes to paying taxes with an LLC, you can choose how to be taxed, either as sole proprietor or partnership. If you declare yourself an LLC, expect lots of paperwork on both federal and state levels, along with filing fees. Also, some states don't allow LLCs, so check your local options.

GOING INTO BUSINESS WITH A LOVED ONE

Maybe your ideal dream business involves you working with a spouse or your best friend. If so, you'll need to take special care that you both want the same things. Making job descriptions for yourself or for each other is key. Being very specific about who is going to do what and when is paramount to the success of your business and the stress level for each of you. Honesty will be your biggest business commodity, and you'll need to treat the care and feeding of not only your joint venture but also your relationship with the utmost respect.

Also, if you're considering going into business with a pal, a partnership agreement, at the very least, is an absolute must — especially if either one of you is investing personal monies into the business. We've all heard sad, sad horror

FROM THE CREATIVE COLLECTIVE: HEATHER BAILEY

Take the time to set up your business properly. Incorporate, get your business and resale licenses, file your fictitious-name statement (DBA), register trade names and trademarks, and apply for patents. Be ready to grow from the get-go so that you don't have to stop your momentum to take care of the things that should have been in place from the beginning.

stories of two friends, close as can be, whose friendship was ruined by a bad business relationship. Take care to make sure this doesn't happen to you. And to do so, you might want to consult with a lawyer. (More on working with an attorney in chapter 20.)

Before you ask your friend or mother-in-law or whomever to go into business with you, or before you say yes to a business proposal from your personal trainer, favorite barista, or good neighbor, take some time to think long and hard about it before you either (a) ask, or (b) accept.

Here's a list of things to consider:

Are you really interested in collaborating with someone, or do you just prefer not to work alone? If you suspect that you may want your friend on board because you don't like making big decisions by yourself, and you think they always have groovy ideas, perhaps you just need a personal board of directors (page 105) or a mentor (page 94), rather than a partner.

Are your working styles compatible? Just like in your personal life,

it's nice to have a partner who offers you some sort of balance. Your business is a lot like your love life in that regard. If you both dislike packing and shipping and you are always waiting for the other one to do it, well, your wonderful products may never leave your storeroom. Defining just who is going to do what and when is a big deal. Do you think you could work closely with someone who is very different from you? It's important to be honest with yourself here. Brutally, brutally honest. As with personalities, complementary job skills are important.

Why do you want to be in business with this other person? What do they have to offer that your business needs? Conversely, if partnering up is their idea, what do you bring to the table that they desire?

Are you comfortable insisting on getting a lawyer involved? If for some reason you or your perspective partner is leery of lawyers when it comes to your joint partnership, you should see that as a red flag.

SIGNING CONTRACTS

Through the course of owning your business, you may be asked to sign any manner of contracts. If you're licensing your designs or signing a lease or getting insurance, a contract will be involved. Unless you're a superhuman with magical powers, most likely you're going to need some help understanding exactly what it is you're agreeing to.

Save yourself the agony of sleepless nights, second-guessing yourself, and that pit of fear in your stomach. Get legal help! No, most lawyers don't come cheap, but what they can provide for you is almost priceless: peace of mind. Here's the deal. If you're going to sign a complicated contract, especially one that deals with paying you money, get a lawyer or another kind of expert, like an agent, on your team. I insist.

Money, honey: can you talk about it open and honestly? If you're shy talking with your prospective partner about dollars and cents or pounds or euros, you're already in trouble. An open and honest heart-to-heart about the bottom line is definitely in order. If you can't be clear about expectations of money, you shouldn't be in business with another person.

EXERCISE
Make a detailed benefits-and-challenges list about your future partnership. In fact, make several based on these categories and any others you can think of:

➤ Working styles / personalities

➤ Strengths and weaknesses (both your own and your proposed partner's)

➤ Sole ownership of the business

➤ Joint ownership of the business

With the help of your accountant, it's a good idea to determine a percentage of your income goal as your tax burden, and then set that amount aside each month. You may settle on 20 percent or even 33 percent of what you bring in. Immediately put this money into a separate account (the "immediately" part is key) so that when it comes time to pay the tax man and your financial helper, you have the money already set aside.

TAXES

While paying your taxes might not really fit into your business planning, it does need to fit into your business. Most business owners in the United States pay taxes quarterly, and this needs to be budgeted for. Working with a bookkeeper or accountant should help you manage this aspect of your business.

When in doubt, the IRS website (www.irs.gov) is a wonderful resource for all things taxes. Most questions you may have about paying your business taxes can be answered there, and they also have many useful free tools that you can access. I frequently rely on their tax estimator.

I meet countless people who are shocked when their taxes come due and then struggle to pay them, creating a hardship with either their business or personal accounts. I recommend avoiding this at all costs!

PAYROLL

Sweet! You have an employee! Being the boss of someone aside from yourself is a big deal! Possibly you're just working with a virtual assistant from a far-off land, but whatever the case may be, there are laws about paying your people. Your bookkeeper or accountant should be able to help you with this; you can also contact your local government offices to find out what is required of you as an employer. This is one area of your business that you don't want to mess around with. Employee issues are a part of your business where it can be useful to get some legal help.

WORKPLACE RULES AND REGS

Developing your personnel policies and work expectations is a big responsibility. Hammering out the details of everything from your employee manual or guidelines to making sure your workplace is safe and up to code can be time consuming. But you have to do it. Knowing what you can expect from anyone you hire and what you're responsible for if they should leave your company, by choice or not, is an area where you may need to get professional guidance. You'll need to be aware and familiar with the employment laws for your locale.

Are you going to be responsible for paying your employee's sick days or vacation time? Do you have a system in place for scheduling and requesting time off? Does your employee understand their job description? Does your insurance policy cover them having keys to your operation? Or would you be better off working with someone on a contract basis? I suggest that you consult with your local Small Business Administration office before you decide to add a paid worker to your team. Many local chambers of commerce even offer classes to members to help navigate the ins and outs of being an employer.

PAYING FOR HELP = BIG PAYOFF

Lots of times, hiring someone is a great way to grow your business. You are only one person, and I hope you know: You can only do so much. You can only be so much. You can only produce so much. And that's OK. Your business can be as small as you like or grow as big as you want. If you feel like you could be expanding or making more money if only you had some help, investigate it. Hiring extra hands enabled these Creative Collective business owners to get back to what they love best, which in most cases is creating.

"I reached a point where I hit a ceiling as far as my individual earning potential. I was already working as many hours as I could, with the highest-paying clients I could, and I was turning away business to the tune of $40,000 a year just because I didn't have the manpower to fulfill the orders. I was so afraid of hiring help because I didn't understand the tax implications and increased costs, and then I met a wonderful business adviser who took every worry off of my shoulders. She now manages all of my payroll and taxes, and today I have two full-time employees I couldn't imagine working without. The cost of hiring an employee is justified for me when they are able to bring in more money than they cost, and I knew that when I hit that ceiling of growth I had to reach out and accept some help. The benefits since I began hiring have been immeasurable in ways I never expected — the collaboration, the emotional investment each worker has in our collective success, and the sheer amount of ideas and

inspiration that we are able to generate together is invaluable."
— MEGAN HUNT

"Even if you have the skill set to do it all, you will never have the time. Focus on what is most important and delegate what you can. Carefully assess what is a good use of your time."
— HEATHER BAILEY

"I realize that I can't grow beyond where I am right now without some help, so I see hiring an employee as an investment in the growth of my business. I want my business to grow much bigger than it is now, and I know I can't do it alone!"
— JESSICA SWIFT

INSURANCE

Bottom line on insurance is that you most likely need it. If you have a space where clients or customers come to you — even if it's your home where you do custom dress fittings, and even if your clients are most likely going to be friends of yours or your family — you need to protect yourself, and you can do that best by having an insurance policy. You need to be protected for any number of reasons, and, yes, most of them are scary. Someone could trip and fall climbing the stairs to your studio, breaking a leg. Or maybe someone is highly allergic to an ingredient in your world-famous oatmeal raisin cookies and goes into anaphylactic shock. It doesn't matter what the reason is; you need to make sure that your business is protected and in some cases your personal assets are protected, too.

You can check to see if your homeowner's or renter's insurance covers you, but in most instances you'll need additional coverage. If you're thinking of getting a store or studio space, your landlord or even your town, county, or state may *require* that you're insured, so you'll have no choice in the matter.

INSURANCE TERMS AND WHAT THEY MEAN

Let's learn a bit about insurance basics, which means knowing the lingo.

- **Liability:** This means risk. Anything that can put your business at risk is liability. Like if you use dangerous equipment, it can be considered a liability.

- **Liability insurance:** Liability insurance is there to protect you in case you are sued.

- **Product liability insurance:** If you make a product that could potentially cause harm to someone, you may want to check into having this type of insurance. This is good for people who work with food, lotions, or dinnerware.

- **Business income insurance:** This kind of insurance can help you if your business suffers a property loss like a flood or fire, anything that forces your business to shut down for any length of time.

- **Property insurance:** Whether you rent or own, this insurance can cover your property in case of a damaging event. This can help you recoup the loss of property as well as inventory.

- **Policy:** This is what your whole agreement is called, from the contracts you sign to the services you're paying your insurance company for.

HEALTH INSURANCE

While we're on the topic of insurance, I'd like to mention health insurance. For many self-employed people in the United States, what to do about health insurance is a big question and often a factor in how far we push our businesses. If you can't rely on a partner to supply your personal health insurance, you'll need to find it somewhere else and figure out how to pay for it, which can be confusing and daunting, to say the least.

If you were very recently employed and offered coverage, or you are employed now and have coverage, check with your human resources department to find out what your COBRA options are. COBRA stands for Consolidated Omnibus Budget Reconciliation Act, and if you work for a large company, usually you are offered the opportunity to carry your insurance over after you leave your job, though, granted, usually at much higher rates than you were paying when you were employed. If your company offers COBRA, it can be worth checking into, especially if you are responsible for insuring other people besides yourself. Plug that number into your budget and see how it works. This is an option and sometimes it's your only one.

Some states, like mine, require that all residents carry some kind of personal health insurance, and therefore the state has many options one can choose from. Check out your state's official website for information on guarantors they have partnerships with and then begin making phone calls.

Also, don't overlook professional organizations you are associated with. For example, as a published author, I could carry dental and health insurance from my professional writers' organization.

I truly wish there was an easy answer to the dilemma of health insurance. But sadly there isn't, at least not as of this writing in the United States. Research the options in your state or country, get quotes from companies, and understand what you're paying for. Good luck!

BEST INSURANCE BANG FOR THE BUCK

Like anything else business related, settling on an insurance policy will take research and time. You need to be sure of and understand completely what you're getting for your money. The best way to find a company that you'll like working with is to ask for recommendations. Check with other business owners you know and ask them for referrals.

Chapter 20

PROFESSIONAL SUPPORT
AND WHERE TO FIND IT

When it comes to hiring anyone to assist you with creating your incredible business, you now know that you'll need to hire help. Be it a website designer or a logo designer, an insurance agent or a licensing agent, an attorney or a bookkeeper, hiring help is an important job.

ACCOUNTANTS AND LAWYERS AND AGENTS, OH MY!

Just how are you supposed to go about hiring these fine folks when you're meant to be, or would much rather be, creating your products or services? Just as you invest your money, you have to invest your time.

Start with people you know who may be already using these service professionals. Ask them for recommendations and referrals. A tip-top referral can go a long way when it comes to your peace of mind. You can also check with your local Small Business Administration, chamber of commerce, mentor, or mastermind group. Or do the new-fashioned thing and conduct Internet searches.

Once you find several candidates you're interested in, research them thoroughly. While your neighbor may highly recommend her agent, lawyer, or bookkeeper, you need to do further investigation to make sure that they'll be just as good a match for you. Google them and check with the Better Business Bureau for any reports that may have been filled against them.

When their background check checks out, contact them and request a meeting to discuss your needs. Make sure you determine ahead of time if you'll be charged for this initial meeting. Usually informative meetings that may lead to long-term business relationships are free, but

FROM THE CREATIVE COLLECTIVE: **KRISTEN RASK**

I highly suggest getting a bookkeeper right away! It might seem daunting to hire someone, but they can help you learn about your books so you end up paying less. You should have a good understanding of your finances.

don't leave this to chance. There is nothing like sitting down with a business professional for what you think is a meet-and-greet only to be charged $85 when you walk out the door. This actually happened to a friend of mine.

GETTING TO KNOW ALL ABOUT YOU...

Before meeting with a potential professional helpmate, have a thoroughly researched list of questions to ask. If you're not sure what questions to ask, head to your friendly fellow businesspeople and query them about what they wished they had asked these professionals before they had hired them. Or based on what they know now, what do they wish they had known then?

Some jumping-off points:

» How do they charge for their services?

» How is it best to be in touch with them?

» How long can you expect it to take for them to respond when you have questions or concerns about something?

» Do they charge for phone consultations/questions?

LEGAL ANSWERS ON THE CHEAP

Check your area for organizations like Lawyers for the Arts or Volunteer Lawyers for the Arts. Sometimes you can get quick and easy and cheap (or free!) help for your smaller legal issues. Also, if you happen to live near a law school, you might be in luck. Lots of times, these schools offer services at a low(er) cost. I once attended an Ask a Lawyer event at a very prestigious university, where I sat down for 45 minutes with an advanced student of law who answered my questions for free. You can't beat *that* fee!

Though he's an Ohio resident, Michael Elliott is an innovative certified public accountant (CPA) who works with clients remotely all across the United States. He particularly loves helping creative people because they, too, are innovative and interested in utilizing the newest tools and technologies to help grow their businesses. Along with providing accounting and tax work, Michael offers high-level consultancy services by developing personal relationships with his clients, his assumption being that by better understanding his clients' businesses, he can help them grow and succeed. Michael's Q&A session offers insight into how having a numbers maven in your corner can be an asset to any business, old or new, big or small.

How could working with a CPA or bookkeeper benefit my business?
The advantages of working with an accounting professional are twofold. First, they are aware of accounting and tax regulations applicable to your business, so they can provide you with guidance as to the deductibility of certain items as well as how best to organize and present your accounting data. Second, a good accounting professional should be passionate about helping *you* succeed. You need to make sure that you find someone who truly cares about you and about your business. Someone who is willing to go above and beyond the tax return and accounting data to get to the heart and soul of your business. Only when a relationship with your accountant is developed can it really help you transform your business!

Can a numbers person help me with my business planning? If so, how?

Absolutely. Numbers people can be a valuable asset when it comes to business planning and consulting. For me as an accountant, numbers just make sense. When I look at a client's financials, I can see the relationships between their numbers and their business processes. I can often tell more about a person by looking at their tax return than I can by having a simple conversation with them! By looking at numbers, I can easily identify areas for improvement and growth. When choosing an accountant, the real key here is not simply finding a numbers person since they are a dime a dozen; the issue is finding someone who can look at your numbers and transform them into a beautiful roadmap of success for your business *and* communicate this information to you. If they can't, they will be of no use to you in your business.

Can you share with us what we should ask a prospective money person when we're in the market to hire someone?

First of all, look for someone who understands the creative industry. Why? Because accountants are often afraid of the innovation and technology that most creative types demand, so you need to find someone who embraces the excitement and innovation that imaginative individuals bring to their businesses, not be made nervous by it!

Three questions to ask when looking for an accountant are:

1. What do you think about working with creative people like me? Is that something you are comfortable with?
2. How are you going to add value to my business beyond simply completing my accounting and tax work?
3. How are you going to help and encourage me to innovate and grow my business?

Look for an accountant who wants to develop a relationship with you and get to know you so that they can provide more specific and quality services to meet your needs.

What are your top tips for keeping track of records as one's business grows?

Many systems are available for keeping track of your business income and expenses. A very outdated but commonly used system is keeping monthly, quarterly, or yearly receipts in expense-specific file folders. At the end of the period, those receipts are entered into some sort of accounting system. Accounting systems can range from a simple Excel spreadsheet to a full-blown accounting package like QuickBooks, Peachtree, or Quicken.

I believe creative people should use a software package hosted in the cloud (that is, on someone else's server). These types of programs (like Xero and FreshBooks) allow business owners to track and enter receipts as an expense is incurred or as invoices are generated. Some of these programs will even allow you to scan in your receipts and attach them to the applicable expense, eliminating the need to keep the originals! This will enable you to pull up the expense in your program at any time and see exactly what was paid for, along with the exact receipt. Another advantage to these "cloud solutions" is that these programs are always accessible from anywhere in the world (including your favorite

coffee shop), and many of these accounting programs have applications for use on your smartphone. Having an accounting program easily accessible makes it easy to keep up-to-date books.

What, if anything, should be notated on receipts?

I'm a big fan of writing the name of the expense account directly on a receipt. For example, if you purchase several boxes of printer paper, note "Office Supplies" on the receipt, corresponding with this disbursement category on your accounting program's chart. Any meals and entertainment expenses you incur should specify not only that the outlay was a "Meals & Entertainment" expense but also the business purpose of the expense, whom you met with, and what the meeting was regarding. For example, if you met Ms. Candy Apple at the Corner Café for burgers and fries, and you discussed your purchase of Candy's handmade picture frames for you to resell on your website as a package deal with your paintings, write the following on the receipt: "Meals & Entertainment, Ms. Candy Apple, purchase of inventory for resale."

Are computer programs like TurboTax a good investment for me? Are there advantages to working with a live person over these programs?

Programs like TurboTax can be very advantageous; however, take great caution when it comes to your decision regarding year-end tax preparation. This kind of software is best suited for people who know exactly what they are doing when it comes to tax preparation and who are very comfortable both with classifying and organizing their income and expenses and understanding and interpreting the Internal Revenue Code (a.k.a. "the Code"). Understanding the Code can be a very challenging undertaking as it is continually changing and adapts to new legislation passed by Congress. Many changes are not put into law until near the end of the year, so it's essential to be constantly up to date on these changes and understand which one will affect your business.

Accounting professionals, on the other hand, have constant access to updates in the Code and related IRS forms via research software and newsletters. Professionals are able to tell immediately what specific portions of the tax-law changes will impact your business. Also, professionals have experience filing many similar tax returns and can apply that specific knowledge to making sure that your return is prepared correctly.

Furthermore, an accountant who is comfortable working in creative industries will know to ask you very specific questions to ensure that your business takes full advantage of all applicable deductions.

How can we keep the IRS happy while improving our bottom line?
The IRS is always happiest when taxpayers take conservative positions for which there is sufficient, appropriate documentation. In English: You can only deduct legitimate business expenses; you can't deduct your groceries or your manicures. And, yes, I have seen both, which is a major tax-deduction fail! The tax man simply wants to ensure that you are reporting all of your receipts and only taking expenses for those items for which you have actually incurred business expenses. The tax man is always happiest when your funds are *not* "comingled." Many people I know think, "Heck, it's all my money, anyway, so what difference does it make what pocket it comes out of?" While I'm not disagreeing that perhaps it's all your money, the IRS likes all business monies deposited in a business account and all business expenses paid out of a business-specific bank account. The whole issue of comingling funds is one that can be very confusing but is vitally important to avoid when ensuring that you stay in compliance with applicable rules and regulations. Which is to say: You really should keep your business and personal monies separate!

In terms of improving your bottom line, make sure that you are taking every possible deduction you are entitled to. If you use something primarily for business, by all means take an expense deduction for it. If you have any questions regarding the deductibility of a specific item, ask a professional. That's what we're here for!

I always thought I'd have to sit down across a desk with someone to make a professional relationship like this succeed. Yet you work with people long distance. How does that operate?
A common misconception is that you have to live right down the road from your accountant. To that I say NO WAY! Choosing an accountant has to do with finding someone you are comfortable with and who understands you and your business. You need a competent individual who is willing to invest time into your business not to pad *their* bottom line, but to help you grow so you can pad *yours*. Where that person has a physical office is completely inconsequential.

You can create this type of remote relationship by utilizing such technologies as online meeting rooms, remote web sessions, and remote communication, including email, Skype, and even good old-fashioned phone calls. All relevant files can be transferred electronically, and the Internet allows me to stay in constant communication with my clients. If your current records are too old-school to be transferred electronically, accountants working remotely can even help you set up an online accounting program that will allow you to work from anywhere — and more efficiently.

How "more efficiently"?
Working remotely not only lets accountants provide more timely services to our clients in a much more effective manner, we can also help a client better manage their time because this eliminates countless trips back and forth to the accountant's office to drop off and/or explain various tax and accounting items. A simple email or webcam session will do the trick, instead.

Incidentally, another common misconception relating to working with a remote accountant is that the accountant wouldn't be familiar with applicable state and local laws. But with the development of advanced tax software and research programs, remote accountants are easily able to adapt to any state or local municipality tax laws.

The future is here, and the future is online! If you explore the option of an online relationship with your accountant, you will find potential cost savings, increased attention from your accountant, value-added services, and, most importantly, a much deeper relationship with the person who is best suited to help you figure out how to make your business successful.

How difficult will it be for me or any other creative individual to find a qualified accountant who will understand my type of business?

When evaluating their accounting and tax preparation options, creative-business owners should be asking several important questions:

» What am I really paying my hard-earned cash to an accountant for?
» What value is my current accountant providing me in my business?
» How could my business benefit from using an accountant who understands my business perhaps better than I do?

Finding a good fit will take some research. Look for an accountant who isn't simply pumping out tax returns but who both understands your business and truly cares about your success, businesswise and personally. Creative individuals need to make sure that they are working with people who will encourage them to use their creativity to enhance and adapt their business processes to our changing world. Your want someone who's willing to be innovative to make your businesses more successful. When you find that type of accountant, with the knowledge and the resources you need to become a successful business owner, your business will really begin to take off!

Q&A WITH
BUSINESS ATTORNEY
BETTIE NEWELL

Bettie is one of the most amazing women I know. She is supersmart, creative, fun to be with, and speaks legalese as her second language. This is someone who seemingly does it all. She volunteers with her local creative community; is a successful photographer; is the mother to two amazing young ladies; and provides counsel to businesses ranging from solo creative ventures to large corporations. Having Bettie in my personal and professional life is a real treat. I asked her to give us the lowdown on the law 'cause, hey, the fine print matters.

How can creative-business people best utilize the services of an attorney?

An attorney can be a great resource for a business owner at any point from starting up through closing a business. Litigators are called on to help resolve disputes, whereas a business lawyer works with her clients to try to *prevent* mistakes from happening and keep them out of a courtroom. While establishing a relationship with a lawyer may not be high on your list of priorities for your business, taking the time to work with a lawyer before you move forward on certain types of projects will likely save you time and money down the road. Lawyers can provide advice on tax and liability issues, employment questions, and many other areas. They can review, draft, and negotiate contracts; help you come up with forms to streamline your day-to-day operations; and are a great source of referrals for other professionals or services your business might need.

Why would a business owner want or need to hire a business lawyer?
Besides the obvious event (if you find yourself in the unfortunate scenario of being sued), there are key places along a business's development where hiring an attorney makes sense. It is beneficial to consult with an attorney while you are in the planning stages of starting a business. An attorney can help you choose the best structure for your business (a sole proprietorship or an LLC, for example), assist with any state and local filings, and help you navigate the tax implications of your chosen structure. An owner should also consider hiring an attorney when entering into contracts, hiring employees, borrowing money (or taking on a partner or investor), and when selling the business.

Can a business attorney help with business planning?
Yes! Your lawyer has counseled other businesses, both large and small, and has likely read many business plans. While she may not be familiar with your specific industry or market, a business lawyer can provide practical advice and be a good sounding board as you plan for the future of your endeavor.

When forming a partnership with a like-minded creative partner, why would someone want or need to have a contract drawn up to protect oneself?
Partnerships are surprisingly easy to form and are sometimes even done inadvertently. When setting out on a collaborative venture, often both parties are so excited, so like-minded, that nobody is thinking anything could ever go wrong. But things *do* go wrong. Going through the exercise of putting together a collaboration or partnership agreement can help turn up issues before they become a problem. Potential partners should discuss and agree on things like what each person will be responsible for doing, how expenses will be paid, how they will make decisions, what happens if one of the partners doesn't fulfill her end of the bargain, and who owns the product and intellectual property they created.

Why is it important to trademark things? And what kind of things should we consider trademarking?
People are often confused between trademarks, copyrights, and patents. All are designed to protect "intellectual property" (inventions of the mind), but they each cover a different area. A trademark protects your brand name and logos (words, phrases, or designs that distinguish your product and brand from someone else's), a copyright protects your original artistic works, and a patent protects your inventions or discoveries.

While it isn't *necessary* to register a trademark to establish that you have rights to that mark, owning a federal trademark registration is advantageous because it puts others on notice that you claim ownership in the mark and creates a legal presumption that you have ownership rights and the exclusive right to use that mark in the United States.

Before hiring a lawyer, what are some questions one should always ask to make sure that person is a good fit for them?
One of the most important things to find out is what the billing arrangement will be. Ask your attorney what her hourly rate is (or whether the project will be done on a fixed fee), if she charges for administrative tasks (like copying and faxing), whether a retainer is required, and how often you will be billed.

That being said, don't hire a lawyer just because she is the cheapest one you can find. It's important to work with someone you feel comfortable with and who (preferably) has some experience working with small creative businesses. Find out what sort of work she has done in the past — most lawyers have online biographies or can provide you with a résumé.

The best place to start when looking for a lawyer is with personal referrals. Ask friends and colleagues in your geographic area if they have someone they would recommend. Once you have some names, set up an initial consultation and come armed with questions.

Why is it recommended that an attorney be involved when signing a lease on a retail or studio space?
Commercial leases are often pre-printed forms full of legalese, and landlords may not be willing to negotiate the terms. Even so, it is a good idea to have an attorney review the provisions in the contract so that you know *exactly* what you are getting into.

Is there a difference between a lawyer and an attorney?
No, the distinction is meaningless. A person licensed to practice law in any state in the union may refer to themselves as either a lawyer or an attorney. I happen to like the word attorney more, but when someone asks me what I do for a living, I invariably refer to myself as a business lawyer.

What else should we know about working with legal counsel?
Don't be intimidated by the thought of hiring a lawyer. We're regular people who survived law school and one or more state bar exams and sometimes just happen to work in very fancy offices. Consider your lawyer an important, practical member of your team who can provide support and assistance for many of the questions that will arise in your business.

FROM THE CREATIVE COLLECTIVE: HEATHER BAILEY

Take the time to get agreements in writing. It can be time consuming, expensive, and uncomfortable to spell out the details of a relationship, but making expectations clear upfront can save money, dispel conflict, and even prevent heartache down the line. When difficulties arise, the larger the sum of money that's at stake, the greater each view of what was promised can vary.

PARTING ADVICE

I'll let some members of the Creative Collective have the last word — or words — seeing as how these highly successful people clearly know what they're talking about.

JESSICA SWIFT

My top business-planning advice is to take some time at the end of each year to do a review of everything that went well in your business, everything that you accomplished, all the ideas that you have for where you'd like your business to go . . . everything. Spend some of this time visualizing and fantasizing wildly about what your dream business looks like. I think having a big end goal to visualize helps you move down your path in a focused way. Use that vision as a gauge for what you do in your business. Allow that vision to change and morph and grow as your business grows. Don't look at it as a static image that will never change; use it as something that you get to interact with, to inspire you and keep you excited about where your business is going!

DEB THOMPSON

Approach all aspects of your business with integrity: relationships, employees, money, clients, artists, vendors.

JOLIE GUILLEBEAU

I'm still getting used to the idea of calling myself a businessperson. I really resisted the idea of "business" for a long time. Instead of thinking of my work as "building a business," I consider it "building my own security." I made a visual metaphor: a house. Each wall represents one aspect of my plan for security: selling prints, originals and daily paintings, shows and art fairs, and teaching. I work at building each wall slowly.

MICHELLE WARD

When it comes to your business, nobody knows it better than you do.

ALEXANDRA FRANZEN

I believe in the power of underpromising and overdelivering. And to accomplish that, it's often wise to undercommit, at least until you've got a very clean and clear grip on how long certain tasks will *really* take you to complete.

MEGAN AUMAN

I can't say I would have done anything differently. Even the mistakes I've made in my business were all tremendous learning opportunities, and I don't think I'd be where I am today without them.

KRISTEN RASK

I am a firm believer in starting small and growing from there. I think those who invest significant time and money on a business have a greater chance of going under faster since they don't have much of a cushion to get them through the slow or hard times.

ACKNOWLEDGMENTS

I'd first like to thank everyone who has supported *The Handmade Marketplace: How to Sell Your Crafts Locally, Globally, and Online.* I am full of gratitude from the bottom of my heart to every single person who came to a signing; attended one of my workshops; left an online review of the book; blogged about it; tweeted it; joined the page on Facebook; and most of all, supported me by buying the book. I've always been a huge believer in community, and all of you have made me feel so welcome and at home in your worlds. Thank you so, so much.

Right after my readers, the person I owe a huge thanks to is one Ms. Holly Bemiss, my agent. She is amazing, wonderful, creative, and patient — and has lovely hair. Thank you to Erin Bried for meeting me for pancakes and then introducing me to Holly.

Have you ever known someone who just makes your creative wheels turn and just looking at them fills you with good ideas and inspiration? For me, one of those people is Deborah Balmuth, editorial director at Storey. A cup of coffee with her can be life changing.

Speaking of Storey, I'd like to mention Pam Art; Amy Greeman; Alee Marsh; and Alethea Morrison; and my editor, freelancer Dale Evva Gelfand. I'm a big fan of all of them.

Thank you to the people who keep me laughing and motivated on a daily basis: Minna Wallace; Shelia Wisenborn-Broderick; Karolyn Tregembo, and her children Benjamin, Nathan, and Joshua; Stephen Wade; Amanda

Struse; Elizabeth Holt; Alana Chernila; Kerri Wessel; Alexandra Lincoln; Nikki Gardner; and Karie Sutherland.

As always, my family is a wonderful source of support. Thanks to my father, Ron, and my wonderful stepmother, Robyn Chapin; my sister, Euretta; and my mother-in-law, Sharon Jandrow. I especially owe a big thank-you to my mother, Janis McWayne, who cheered me on every day through countless email chats and who lent me her house in Vermont to complete this book. Thank you, Mom, for the green juice, long walks, intervals, and all the much-needed porch time and farmers'-markets distractions.

My happiness and motivation are guaranteed by a steady diet of Neko Case, National Public Radio, green smoothies, and Abraham-Hicks. I also owe a debt of gratitude to Dread Euphoria and Meekins Library, both located in Williamsburg, Massachusetts. Ladies of Meekins, thank you so much for all you do for my community and my family.

Last but never, ever least, I'd like to thank my husband, Eric. I love our whole life so much. I am so grateful for you every single day, every minute, every second. I would not have finished this book, or anything else I've ever begun since we met, without you being on my team. I have a lot of other mushy, nice things to say about you, but I want to say them to your face. Come find me, I'm probably reading a book on our lovely porch with our dogs nearby.

RESOURCES

Here are some resources for you to further explore. The Creative Collective has provided me with endless inspiration, and I hope that you will take a closer look at each of their websites, which I know you'll not only enjoy but perhaps also find motivation for growing your own business. I would like to thank each and every one of them for the invaluable contributions they made to *Grow Your Handmade Business*. If you were inspired or moved by anything you learned from them here, please let them know!

THE CREATIVE COLLECTIVE

Abby Kerr
www.abbykerrink.com

Alexandra Franzen
www.alexandrafranzen.com

Alison Lee
www.craftcast.com

Bettie Newell
www.littlepapercities.com

Deb Thompson
www.nahcotta.com
www.enormoustinyart.com

Heather Bailey
www.heatherbailey.typepad.com

Jay McCarroll
www.jaymccarrollonline.com

Jena Coray
www.missmodish.com
www.modishblog.com

Jennifer Lee
www.artizencoaching.com
www.rightbrainbusinessplan.com

Jessica Swift
www.jessicaswift.com

Jessie Oleson
www.cakespy.com

Jolie Guillebeau
www.jolieguillebeau.com

Karie Sutherland
www.orderaheadorganizing.com

Kelly Rae Roberts
www.kellyraeroberts.com

Kristen Rask
www.schmancytoys.com

Lisa Congdon
www.lisacongdon.com

Megan Auman
http://designinganmba.com

Megan Hunt
www.princesslasertron.com
www.campcoworking.com

Michael Elliott
www.geaugacpa.com

Michelle Ward
www.whenigrowupcoach.com

Nicole Balch
www.makingitlovely.com

Rebecca Pearcy
www.queenbee-creations.com
www.rebeccapearcy.com
www.chickpeababy.com

Sue Eggen
www.giantdwarfdesign.com

Tara Gentile
www.taragentile.com
www.scoutiegirl.com

CROWD-FUNDING WEBSITES

Kickstarter, Inc.
www.kickstarter.com

Indiegogo, Inc.
www.indiegogo.com

Invested.in
www.invested.in

KARI'S MENTORS

Martha Beck
www.marthabeck.com

Martha Stewart
www.marthastewart.com

ONLINE PRODUCTIVITY TOOLS

Freckle
www.letsfreckle.com
Software for tracking time usage

The Pomodoro Technique
www.pomodorotechnique.com
For managing blocks of time

ONLINE PROJECT-MANAGEMENT TOOLS

Springpad
www.springpadit.com

TeuxDeux
www.teuxdeux.com

Trello
www.trello.com

LEGAL AND GOVERNMENT RESOURCES

For readers in the United States: to find lawyers in your state, simply Google your state + "Lawyers for the Arts"

Creative Commons
www.creativecommons.org

Internal Revenue Service
www.irs.gov

SCORE Association
www.score.org

U.S. Small Business Administration
www.sba.gov

INDEX

PRAISE FOR THE FIRST BEST-SELLING BOOK BY KARI CHAPIN

"Thanks to this terrific book, I am prepared to make a fortune selling my googly-eyed peanuts. After spending countless hours scouring flea markets and craft fairs, it's fascinating to see how things work on the other side of the table."
— **AMY SEDARIS**

"Kari has thoughtfully created the very best guidebook for navigating the craft marketplace. Her personal voice, guided by personal experience is evident throughout the book. You'll feel encouraged, inspired, and informed . . . totally confident to jump start your own craft business!"
— **AMY BUTLER, AMY BUTLER DESIGN**

"This book has an eye to making a living through your craft rather than making money on the side. It is a detailed and intensive bootcamp for getting a business up and running and keeping it successful through marketing — all wrapped up in an adorable package, charming illustrations and a 'please hold me' size."
— **KNITTY.COM**